T0358216

Cambridge Elements ≡

Elements in Public and Nonprofit Administration
edited by
Andrew Whitford
University of Georgia
Robert Christensen
Brigham Young University

NEW PUBLIC GOVERNANCE AS A HYBRID

A Critical Interpretation

Laura Cataldi
*University of Eastern Piedmont
"Amedeo Avogadro"*

Shaftesbury Road, Cambridge CB2 8EA, United Kingdom

One Liberty Plaza, 20th Floor, New York, NY 10006, USA

477 Williamstown Road, Port Melbourne, VIC 3207, Australia

314–321, 3rd Floor, Plot 3, Splendor Forum, Jasola District Centre,
New Delhi – 110025, India

103 Penang Road, #05–06/07, Visioncrest Commercial, Singapore 238467

Cambridge University Press is part of Cambridge University Press & Assessment,
a department of the University of Cambridge.

We share the University's mission to contribute to society through the pursuit of
education, learning and research at the highest international levels of excellence.

www.cambridge.org
Information on this title: www.cambridge.org/9781009454032

DOI: 10.1017/9781009418904

First published 2024

A catalogue record for this publication is available from the British Library.

ISBN 978-1-009-45403-2 Hardback
ISBN 978-1-009-41892-8 Paperback
ISSN 2515-4303 (online)
ISSN 2515-429X (print)

New Public Governance as a Hybrid

A Critical Interpretation

Elements in Public and Nonprofit Administration

DOI: 10.1017/9781009418904
First published online: January 2024

Laura Cataldi
University of Eastern Piedmont "Amedeo Avogadro"
Author for correspondence: Laura Cataldi, laura.cataldi@uniupo.it

Abstract: This Element focuses on New Public Governance as one of the major administrative narratives of our times. It offers a critical interpretation of NPG as a hybrid tool for management, governance, and reform, arguing that NPG coexists with and is likely to gradually merge into New Public Management. Several arguments support the "continuity and hybridization" hypothesis, whereby the transition from NPM to NPG occurred through the retention of key elements and a layering and sedimentation process. These arguments challenge the "linear substitution" hypothesis, accounting for NPM's persistence and dominance. The Element develops a new interpretation of NPG and discusses the challenges that NPG poses. Finally, it shows that exploring hybridity is critical for evaluating the potential of NPG in terms of a shift in public administration and understanding governance trajectories and reform scenarios.

Keywords: new public governance, new public management, hybridization, narratives, state

ISBNs: 9781009454032 (HB), 9781009418928 (PB), 9781009418904 (OC)
ISSNs: 2515-4303 (online), 2515-429X (print)

Contents

1 Introduction

This Element focuses on New Public Governance (NPG) as one of the major administrative narratives of our times. Based on a wide range of existing literature, it offers a critical interpretation of NPG as a "hybrid" narrative object and, specifically, a management, governance, and reform tool. Indeed, it argues that NPG coexists with and is likely to gradually merge into New Public Management (NPM), the competing and hitherto dominant narrative of the public sector's management, governance, and reform.

In this introduction, preliminary definitions of NPM and NPG, as well as "hybridization" and its related concepts, are required and useful.

As Denhardt and Denhardt (2000, 550) write, "the 'New Public Management' refers to a cluster of ideas and practices that seek, at their core, to use private-sector and business approaches in the public sector" (see also Haynes 2003). Instead, NPG "is a holistic, networked approach to the institutional relationships within society to understand, develop, and implement public policy within a pluralist state" (Young et al. 2020, 482).

Regarding "hybridization" and its related terms, definitions could be provided starting from the biological origins of the concepts and drawing from a rapidly expanding body of literature, particularly in the field of public administration and governance (inter al., Aristovnik et al. 2022; Battilana et al. 2017; Brandsen et al. 2005; Brandsen 2010; Denis et al. 2015; Skelcher 2012). Within this context, "hybrids" are objects – entities, organizations, systems, and even narratives – that combine (mix, or blend) elements. These elements include characteristics, features, principles, and logics from different and sometimes contrasting sources, such as models, ideal types, archetypes, paradigms, and, more broadly, worlds and domains. Hybridity is the property of these objects, denoting the state of being hybrid, characterized by the coexistence and combination of diverse components, which can give rise to tensions and possible contradictions (Denis et al. 2015; Glynn et al. 2020). Lastly, hybridization is the (combination, mixing, or blending) process that gives rise to hybridity as a property and a general phenomenon related to hybrid objects. The concept of "hybridity" is distinguished by its processual, as well as broadly "transitional" character (Brandsen 2010, 840), and it opposes the concept of "purity" (Krlev and Anheier 2020). As observed by Brandsen (2010, 840), "in public administration research," hybridity "tends to denote public/private mixes [. . .], whereas in organizational theory it generally refers to combinations of coordination mechanisms such as hierarchies, markets, and networks."

In light of what has been said, hybridization is to be understood, in general, as a process that involves the public sector and occurs between the state, intended as government, as well as "public" and "hierarchy," and what is "other than the state" (i.e., market and networks as "nonpublic," "nongovernmental," and "private" *lato sensu*). However, in this Element, hybridization is more specifically the process that pertains to NPG as an administrative narrative and occurs between NPG and its predecessor, NPM.

Osborne (2006, 377), the inventor of the term NPG and initiator of this new public narrative, provocatively argued that, in public administration and management, "NPM has actually been a transitory stage" in the evolution from Traditional Public Administration (TPA) to NPG, adding that NPM has occupied "a relatively brief" time "between the statist and bureaucratic tradition of PA and the embryonic plural and pluralist tradition of the NPG." After Osborne's article, "great debate ensued among scholars on how NPG should be defined, and how it varies from NPM" (Young et al. 2020, 482).

Undoubtedly, "the considerable variations in observable governance practices attributable to context-specific differences and the choice of analytical categories for describing such practices" (Wiesel and Modell 2014, 201, note 1) make NPG "object" very complex to capture. According to Koppenjan and Koliba (2013, 2), "NPG may be an umbrella concept under which a large variety of governance innovations are assigned that may have little in common." Furthermore, as Liddle (2018, 971) points out, "the concept of NPG has been criticized for its fuzziness and for being used in substantially different ways (as a practical or normative concept) and amidst diverging discussions" in different social sciences fields, including public administration.

Therefore, one of the main objectives of this contribution is to identify a strategy to capture NPG as a narrative object in order to evaluate its potential in terms of a shift in public administration and public sector reforms. For this purpose, it is necessary to discuss the supposedly oppositive nature of NPG to its predecessor NPM, as well as to take an argued position on the scholarly debate about their relationship, engaging with the most significant hypotheses present in the literature. Thus, key research questions are: Is NPM really *passé* (Hyndman and Lapsley 2016) or dead, as some scholars (see Dunleavy et al. 2006) and politicians (see the Danish Social Democratic Prime Minister, Mette Frederiksen – Krogh et al. 2022) argue? Will NPG replace, transform, or coexist with NPM?

The Element argues that, although NPG really has a reactive origin to NPM, its oppositive nature (i.e., its irreconcilability with NPM's fundamental tenets and ideas) has been somehow purposely overemphasized to legitimize the new narrative in the face of the failures of the hitherto dominant narrative, NPM.

Although NPG originated as a counternarrative to NPM, several arguments will be brought to support one of the two major hypotheses in the literature regarding the relationship and transition between NPM and NPG, namely the "continuity and hybridization" one. According to this hypothesis, the transition from NPM to NPG took place through "the retention of key elements" (Wiesel and Modell 2014, 180) found in previous governance models, such as NPM and TPA, largely via a layering and sedimentation process (Mahoney and Thelen 2010; Streeck and Thelen 2005; see also Dickinson 2016; Hyndman and Liguori 2016; Ongaro 2009; Torfing et al. 2020). The coexistence of these "old" elements within NPG in combination with "new" features is precisely what makes NPG a hybrid. These arguments challenge the "linear substitution" hypothesis, whereby a whole new governance perspective has supplanted NPM (Denhardt and Denhardt 2000; Dunleavy et al. 2006; Entwistle and Martin 2005), positing radical change if not subversion. Therefore, the Element, providing an original construction of arguments in favor of the "continuity and hybridization" hypothesis, ultimately endorses the overarching observation of Aristovnik et al. (2022, 3), highlighting that "when a particular new model is embraced, it is not very likely that it will directly replace all of the previous mechanisms, principles, ideas, and practices. Throughout history, new models have emerged, and new developments have accumulated, yet specific trends of the earlier models remain relevant and are now intertwined with the new ideas."

In this context, characterizing NPG as a hybrid means unveiling, beyond rhetoric, its not complete "otherness" from NPM, highlighting elements and reasons for continuity amidst change, and discussing the potential tensions and challenges that NPG as a hybrid poses. This is especially relevant in terms of democratic governance as NPG promises a re-politicization and re-democratization of the public sector after what is widely recognized as a period of destructive dominance by NPM.

Getting involved in a rather heated and populated discussion such as the one on the relationship between NPM and NPG is important to understand the evolutions in governance, public management, and reform processes. So, other research questions, which will be addressed in the conclusions, are: What are the implications of this hybridization process in and between administrative narratives? What governance, administrative and reform scenarios are emerging? In which direction do narratives and reformtrajectories seem to go?

Lastly, two clarifications are needed. First, although this Element considers NPG a "narrative object," it does not propose a typical narrative or discourse study. Instead, it offers a conceptual analysis, built upon an extensive body of literature, of NPG as a narrative tool oriented to the public sector's management, governance, and reform. This analysis is aligned with the perspective of the "interpretive public administration" (Bevir and Rhodes 2022; Needham

2015; Rhodes 2019) as it proposes a (critical and subjective) interpretation and a "story" of other interpretations and "stories" (Bevir and Rhodes 2003, 133; Needham 2015, 340). Second, when considering NPG a narrative object and reform tool, the analysis presented here mainly addresses the world of ideas. Indeed, Jann's (2003, 95–96) *caveat* applies to this Element as well: the contribution "is not about 'real' changes, different 'trajectories' of public sector reform and their outcomes, but about the beliefs, problem definitions and recommended solutions that inspire the 'real' changes or 'trajectories' of public sector reform." Yet, looking at narratives is fundamental not only because "this allows us to mentally map where we have been," that is, "to recognize how we arrived at the situation we are in" and "where we are going to" (Massey 2019, abstract and 9), but also because administrative and governance narratives such as "ideational constructions" have "a real impact on administrative practices and the form and functioning of public organizations" (Torfing et al. 2020, 11), as well as, ultimately, on all of us as citizens.

The Element is structured as follows. After Introduction, Section 2 explains what administrative narratives, like NPG, are and why it is important to look at them as management, governance, and reform tools. Section 3 outlines and discusses the choice of a twofold strategy to "capture" NPG and narrative governance trajectories. The following sections get to the heart of the debate on NPG and its relationship with NPM. Section 4 provides coordinates to understand the NPG object, such as a counternarrative of NPM *in primis*. Section 5 presents the two hypotheses in the literature regarding the relationship between NPG and NPM, taking a position in favor of the "continuity and hybridization" by illustrating sources of continuity and elements that make NPG a hybrid. Sections 6 and 7 outline, respectively, the reasons for NPG hybridization with NPM and NPM persistence/dominance. The concluding sections (8), after a summary of the "NPG as a hybrid" arguments (8.1), highlight the origins and complexities of administrative narratives' hybridity with special reference to NPG (8.2), reflect on the possible reform scenarios (8.3) and, in addition to the dark side and risks of NPG, discuss the conditions for its effectiveness as a democratic model of governance (8.4). Finally, the contribution provides directions for future research (8.5).

2 Administrative Narratives as Management, Governance, and Reform Tools

Since the Element regards NPG as an administrative narrative, this section aims to elucidate what narratives, especially administrative ones, are and to illustrate their significance, underscoring the importance of looking at them.

In public administration, NPG and NPM, together with traditional public administration (TPA), are the major "discursive objects" of our times. In most countries of the world, they inspire both ordinary management (but also policy) practices and reform plans. Andresani and Ferlie (2006, 416) define them as "the two grand narratives of public management reform."

Narratives play a key role in the real world and in public governance since they perform a sense-making function (Weick et al. 2005). As discourses on governing and governance, narratives are storytelling that provide meaning, but also legitimacy and justification, to decision-making, organizations, and policies, supporting their creation, maintenance or change (Magalhães and Amélia Veiga 2018; Wagenaar 2011).

In a discursive and constructivist institutionalist perspective (Hay 2004; Schmidt 2010), narratives are contingent constructs of ideas that, in a continuous and circular dialogue, originate from – and are implemented in – practice (Cataldi and Cappellato 2020). Ultimately, they put at the center the actors' (situated) agency (Bevir and Rhodes 2006; see also Cataldi and Tomatis 2022).

According to Weiss (2020, 106), "narratives are the actual form in which reform ideas become politically relevant"; they are "powerful in political action because actors use stories – deliberately or unconsciously – to transfer information, shape perceptions, develop targets, build coalitions and affect change." It is precisely in this sense that narratives, including administrative ones, are tools in the hands of human agents, and, undoubtedly, crucial actors are the same "narrators."

Due to their human matrix and their connection with real-world practices and events, administrative narratives are complex objects: they are contingent and contextual, as well as susceptible to evolution. Indeed, administrative narratives may have identifiable "initiators" (in the case of NPG, Osborne) but change because – in a continuous circle – they draw inspiration from and nurture changing practices, as well as because they rapidly become and therefore are multivocal coconstructions by scholars, politicians, managers, consultants, and so on. As Torfing et al. (2020, 11) explain, administrative narratives[1] "are not invented out of thin air, but instead are inspired by actual trends" and when they "have first been formulated [. . .] by academic researchers, they quickly attain their own life and provide a [. . .] framework for thinking about and practising public governance. Supporters and advocates help fill in the blanks, and the

---

[1] Instead of narratives, Torfing et al. (2020, 9) use the term "public governance paradigms," since they represent "a relatively coherent and comprehensive set of norms and ideas about how to govern, organize and lead the public sector," and so "a relative unified discourse."

number of specific recommendations grows while key ideas are adapted to new circumstances and new and compatible ideas are integrated."

As Stoker (2006, 43) points out, administrative narratives as management, governance, and reform tools differ in the specific "understanding of human motivation" and "desirability of the emphasis placed on the often competing values of efficiency, accountability, and equity." In fact, "they are called narratives because they are not pure analytical and theoretical frameworks aiming at comprehension (in the Weberian sense): they both mix technical and also political and normative elements" (Ferlie et al. 2009, 12–13). What is crucial, then, is their rhetorical dimension aimed at persuasion and action (or inaction) in the real world (Magalhães and Amélia Veiga 2018, 2).

Torfing and colleagues (2020, 9 and 4) note that administrative and governance narratives, intended as "normative and ideational components of a governance regime," "play an important role as they restructure and reorganize the public sector, change its interactions with the citizens and the private for-profit and non-profit sectors, and transform how public policies, regulations and services are produced, delivered and evaluated." Referring to Kooiman's (2003) conceptual scheme, administrative narratives "provide an instance of 'third-order governance' that creates the normative, ideational and institutional conditions for the structure and processes of the overall system of public governance ('second-order governance'), which in turn conditions the daily interactions and operations through which concrete solutions, regulations and services are produced and delivered ('first-order governance')" (Torfing et al. 2020, 9).

Furthermore, administrative narratives hold and promote different notions of the state (or government) and are characterized by different dilemmas, catchphrases, as well as answers and solutions (Jann 2003). Polzer et al. (2016, 77) highlight how "each administrative paradigm manifests a specific field-level logic [. . .] – that is, bureaucracy (Weberian-style Public Administration), market-capitalism (NPM), and democracy (New Public Governance) – and conveys core ideas of the state, its architecture and role, and its administrative infrastructure." O'Flynn (2007, 353) interprets the paradigmatic narrative changes as "attempts to redefine how we think about the state, its purpose and thus, ways of functioning, operating and managing."

In conclusion, this section highlights the undoubted political and social relevance and significance of administrative narratives as management, governance and reform tools: they are not stories that remain confined to the world of ideas, but by fueling practices and promoting structures and reform plans, they affect people's lives (see inter al. Mintrom and O'Connor 2020).

Finally, a remark: looking at administrative narratives in conjunction with the representations they convey of the state is clearly a way of "bringing political science [but also political sociology and political theory, i.e., more generally, 'the political'] back into public administration research" (Peters et al. 2022), reintegrating "big questions" such as "the capacity and purpose of the state" along with "the big trends shaping the world of governance" (Milward et al. 2016, 312 and 330), and, therefore, taking seriously "the project of reviving PA" and its challenges (Roberts 2018, 82).

3 A Twofold Strategy to "Capture" NPG and Narrative Governance Trajectories

The introduction mentioned that NPG appears challenging to grasp (see, inter al., Koppenjan and Koliba 2013; Liddle 2018). This section, therefore, outlines and justifies what could be described as a twofold strategy to capture NPG.

In this contribution, NPG, as an object of analysis, is treated on two semantic levels. In determining its meaning and content, at the first level, NPG refers to the "original narrative version" that was formalized by Osborne (2006). At the second level, NPG is used as an umbrella term (Koppenjan and Koliba 2013) encompassing other labels, such as "collaborative governance" (Agranoff and McGuire 2003; Ansell and Gash 2008; Bryson et al. 2006), "network governance" (Kickert et al. 1997; Klijn and Koppejan 2000, 2004, 2014), "horizontal/ new governance" (Salamon 2001), but also post-NPM doctrines, such as "joined-up government" (Bogdanor 2005) and "whole-of-government" (Halligan 2006; Christensen and Lægreid 2007a[2]). Furthermore, NPG is often associated with a new public service ethos (Denhardt and Denhardt 2000; Stoker 2006).

While this Element employs both semantic levels for NPG, special emphasis is placed on treating NPG as an umbrella term within the analysis. Indeed, this approach aligns more closely with the concept of administrative narratives as dynamic coconstructions and objects susceptible to evolution.

The choice to treat NPG in this twofold way stems from several considerations. First, referring to the original version of Osborne (2006) makes it possible to define the object of analysis in a sufficiently clear way, avoiding that "the attempts to 'fix' the concept as like trying to 'nail a pudding on the wall'" (Bovaird and Löffler 2003, 316; Pollitt and Bouckhaert 2011, 21). Second, the choice of using NPG as an umbrella term, that includes "twin"

---

[2] In the Element, references to Christensen and Lægreid, sometimes in collaboration with other colleagues, are to be intended as references to leading scholars of post-NPM reforms and governance trajectories. Furthermore, the authors are theorists of governance hybridization. Because of these reasons, they represent an important source of comparison.

narratives (such as collaborative governance) or narratives variously linked by content (e.g., network governance) or time span (post-NPM doctrines, *in primis*), is certainly supported by the fact that many scholars treat NPG as such (inter al. Ingrams et al. 2020; Koppenjan and Koliba 2013; Wiesel and Modell 2014) and/or often as a synonym, subpart or specific evolution of post-NPM (inter al. Aristovnik et al. 2022; Christensen 2012; Dalingwater 2014; Karataş 2019; Robinson 2015; Young et al. 2020).

Robinson (2015, 4 and 9), for instance, argues that "from 2000 there was a discernible trend towards an emerging model variously termed the 'new public service', the 'new public governance' or the 'post-New Public Management' (Dunleavy and Hood, 1994; Denhardt and Denhardt 2000; Osborne 2006)," highlighting how "these approaches do not yet form a coherent paradigm and they have different frames of reference, but some commonalities can be identified that set them apart from earlier traditions and provide the basis for a coherent alternative." Young et al. (2020, 482) write: "Following the NPM movement of the 1990s was the post NPM era, from which the NPG framework evolved." Finally, Aristovnik et al. (2022, 3) state:

> In the literature, we can observe three main pillars in the development of public governance models, starting with traditional models (Weberian public administration and its "Neo" successor), followed by the managerial or market models, the primary representative being New Public Management (NPM), and the third pillar, for which the scientific community has yet to arrive at a consensus. The shifting agenda has seen different emphases for the third pillar – governance, partnerships and networks, transparency, e-government, and the general term post-NPM.

Above all, the choice to treat NPG as an umbrella term (and, therefore, a wider governance model) is motivated by the need to identify an object and, then, a field of analysis that are comprehensive enough to allow a reflection on possible governance trajectories and reform scenarios. In fact, any discussion on possible governance trajectories and reform scenarios requires situating NPG in its broader, both narrative and factual, context. Indeed, the context in which NPG is situated contributes to and continues to define it, both discursively and in practice – for instance, consider the globally transformative role of new digital technologies for society and public administration.

In this perspective, which looks at NPG and, more generally, administrative narratives as "situated," "complex," and "subject to evolution" objects, what Hyndman and Lapsley (2016, 387) say about NPM is also valid about NPG: "Subtle understandings of 'what NPM [in our case, NPG] is' and 'what it is becoming' can be obtained by viewing the NPM [NPG] project as a trajectory rather than as a distinct, static set of ideas at a point in time. This perspective entails both continuity and change."

In the agenda-setting of administrative narratives, timing plays a key role, both as a criterion of (temporal) sorting and a factor of "coagulation" between narratives and narrators: all the narratives under the broad umbrella of NPG draw from the same "primaeval soup" of ideas and policies (Kingdon, 1984) and, by virtue of their coexistence, go through the same process of reciprocal contamination and "softening" that makes them more attractive, and perhaps feasible, to a large community of scholars and practitioners (see Cairney and Zahariadis 2016). Thus, precisely the time variable is one of the essential discriminants for determining the content and extension of the NPG object as a "new administrative and governance model."

However, what to include or not under the NPG umbrella is a choice to be motivated but largely personal. This is in line with the interpretivist recognition of the "inevitability of the 'double hermeneutic' (Giddens 1984)," according to which it is possible to propose only "interpretations of interpretations" (Needham 2015, 340) and "to tell stories about other people's stories" (Bevir and Rhodes 2003, 133), as well as with the idea that this same contribution may be part of the coconstruction process of the NPG narrative.

So, in this Element, not all the narratives contemporaneous with NPG fall under its umbrella, even though they may exhibit similarities with NPG and receive comparable attention because of their ability to address the needs and major changes in society and its governance. For example, as Pollitt and Bouckaert (2011, 19 and 21) observe, among the "more general models offered by academics searching for 'the next big thing'" after NPM, "there are many other varieties, including one that stresses the significance of [. . .] ICTs – this one is termed 'Digital-Era Governance' by its inventors, Dunleavy et al. (2006)," as well as their own suggestion, Neo-Weberian State, "in essence" defined as an "attempt to modernize traditional bureaucracy by making it more professional, efficient, and citizen-friendly." However, in this contribution, both Digital-Era Governance (DEG) and Neo-Weberian State (NWS) were not included among the narratives under the NPG umbrella. The former (DEG) has been excluded because digitalization, beyond its formulation in terms of a quasi-paradigm of public governance proposed by Dunleavy and colleagues (Dunleavy et al. 2006; Margetts and Dunleavy 2013; see also Torfing et al. 2020, chapter 6), seems more a specific mode, a management tool, as well as a reform trajectory or a modernization strategy, serving different governance narratives. The proposal of themes such as reintegrating government and providing holistic services for citizens in response to NPM, as an approach stressing fragmentation, competition and incentivization, would seem to join DEG to NPG and post-NPM. However, digitalization in itself, while undoubtedly important from a reform perspective, represents an expansion and evolution of an NPM trend. In the harsh words of de Vries (2010, 3), "digital-era governance is an (integral) part of the NPM movement." Ultimately, digitalization would seem to rise to a governance paradigm only through a synecdoche mechanism, becoming, in fact, a sort of catch-all narrative. The issue concerning the exclusion of NWS is more complex. The first reason is connected to its genesis: the NWS narrative is not born with an ideally global afflatus like NPG, but from a classification of the governance trajectories in the different countries and, more precisely, as a reform model of the continental European modernizer countries (see also Lynn 2008). A second reason is that, for its own inventors, NWS represents an ideal type substantially different from NPG (and NPM), since it has a different theoretical identity and driving principle. Bouckhaert (2022, abstract) writes: "Next to New Public Management and New Public Governance, the neo-Weberian state also remained a crucial ideal type, certainly for the Western European practice which is embedded in Weberian public administration." He then concludes: "We claim and hypothesise that NWS, much better and even contrary to NPM (market-driven) and NPG (network-driven), will ensure the three core functions of a whole of government strategy within a whole of society context: performing, inclusive and equitable service delivery, resilient crises governance, and effective innovation for government and society" (Bouckhaert 2022, 24). A further reason for the exclusion of NWS is that including it under the umbrella of the "new administrative and governance big thing" (Pollitt and Bouckaert 2011) would require a shift in focus from NPG to an even broader container where post-NPM is not a set of doctrines such as "joined-up government" and "whole-of-government" but "the big umbrella." Exploring post-NPM as "the big umbrella" is certainly an important future research path, but it goes beyond the objectives of this contribution. However, the analysis of NPG in its broader context is an important initial step in this direction.

4 NPG as a Counternarrative: NPG vs. NPM

This section provides coordinates to understand NPG as a narrative "object," outlining its contents and proposals starting from its critique of NPM, thus positioning it as a counternarrative *in primis*.

Several authors present NPG as a reactive response to NPM's flaws and failures (see inter al. Osborne 2006; Fattore et al. 2012), including fragmentation, but also the inability to address "the pervasiveness of wicked problems"

(Torfing et al. 2020, 15; about post-NPM and wicked problems, see Christensen and Fan 2016, 2), such as issues that do not have a definitive solution within the traditional toolbox (Head and Alford 2015), like poverty, unemployment, climate change, public health, and organized crime.[3]

The main criticism directed at NPM is the assimilation to the market and the private sector: "governing is not the same as shopping or more broadly buying and selling goods in a market economy" (Stoker 2006, 46). NPM "has been blamed for [. . .] its belief in individual self-interest as a key guiding principle and its strong reliance on markets as a core steering mechanism," as well as "for its focus on individual rights rather than collective rights" (Van de Walle and Hammerschmid 2011, 191). Moreover, NPM has been criticized for the excessive rationalistic imprinting of its processes and the almost exclusive attention to efficiency rather than effectiveness and equity (Girotti 2007; Capano et al. 2015). As Hood and Dixon (2015b, 265) write, perhaps "the commonest view among students of government is the 'get-what-you-pay-for' view that NPM reforms put too much emphasis on cost cutting and in the process damaged some traditional and important 'Weberian' qualities of administration such as fairness and consistency, the careful framing and application of rules." A generally detected problem is that NPM focuses on (bureaucratic) outputs rather than on (societal) outcomes. Indeed, NPM would be one-dimensional, as it addresses exclusively public bureaucracy management, rather than plural relations with the other main actors of policy implementation structures (Osborne 2006, 2010). Furthermore, one of the most serious unexpected consequences of managerial innovations is the already mentioned fragmentation (as well as siloization) due to the disaggregation and agencification (but also privatization) strategies promoted by NPM (see, inter al. Osborne 2010; Torfing et al. 2012; Van de Walle and Hammerschmid 2011, 194). As Van de Walle and Hammerschmid (2011, 194) explain, "one of the key recommendations of the NPM-movement was to disaggregate large, multifunctional public bodies and replace them with a series of single-purpose bodies." Indeed, "the philosophy was that a deliberate fragmentation and distribution of functions would result in clear lines of control and boundaries and possibly to competition

---

[3] For a critique of the concept of wicked problems as a "fad" in policy analysis and for a reflection on the risks of conceptual stretching (Sartori 1970), see Peters (2017). For the connected issue of the "rhetoric of complexity," see Davies and Chorianopoulos (2018, 3). The two scholars argue that "the point is not to deny that many social phenomena are complex. It is rather that an appropriate theory of governance should problematize complexity. Are phenomena necessarily as complicated as we are encouraged to believe? Which political actors mobilize discourses of complexity for what reasons? Governance theory could also pay more attention to the ways that governing elites and theorists alike avow things to be simple when it suits them, amplifying or reducing complexity to exercise agenda control."

between these new entities." Yet, "disaggregation became fragmentation at the detriment of institutional development" and, more generally, at the expense of public sector coordination. Ultimately, some scholars have observed that the managerialization of the public sector failed in achieving its main promise, also contained in the three Es slogan, that is, "doing more with less" or "to make the government 'run better' and 'cost less'" (Box et al. 2001, 614; Hood and Dixon 2015a; Pollitt and Bouckaert 2004, 8), instead reducing the quality of services and increasing social inequality (Boyne et al. 2003). So, for example, "the story of the NPM era in the United Kingdom is indeed one of 'cost more, worked worse'" (i.e., the "nightmare" outcome), instead of "creating a government that works better and costs less" (i.e., the "dream" outcome) like in the famous title of the United States 1993 National Performance Review report (see Hood and Dixon 2015a, 13 – table 1.1; Hood and Dixon 2015b, 267).

The criticism against NPM is especially harsh among welfare scholars: NPM's managerial ideology, as a "reflection of the powerful dominance of market capitalism over the world" (Tsui and Cheung 2004, 437–438), would be a neoliberal product which has led to the marketization of welfare systems (Clarke 1996). In fact, the introduction of market competition into the public services production – through separation of purchaser/regulatory and provider roles, creation of quasi-markets among public agencies, firms and not-for-profit organizations in health care, education, personal social services, social housing, and so on, and compulsory competitive tendering and market testing (Clark 1996, Figure 2, 24) – would have led users to no longer be clients, but consumers and customers; operators to be bureaucrats instead of professionals; welfare services to be like service companies, where quality is equated with standardization, output orientation is the primary action criterion, and there is a sort of obsession with performance measurement (see Tsui and Cheung 2004). Finally, many authors have advanced concerns about the implications of the "(super)market state model" conveyed by NPM (Van de Walle and Hammerschmid 2011, 196) and its "democraticness" also at the substantive level, as it is "very weak in its notions of citizenship and community" and provides "seemingly apolitical" solutions, avoiding addressing the social issues and structural inequalities that affect society (Box et al. 2001, 613 and 614).

Against this background, NPG's narrative promises a substantial re-democratization and re-politicization of the public sector, advocating several shifts (see Girotti 2007): from within the public administration (i.e., from the bureaucratic organization) to its outside; from the problems of administrative management to those of policymaking, including policy implementation (Osborne 2006); from efficiency to effectiveness; from disaggregation to coordination and integration; from competition to collaboration between public agencies, public and private sectors, profit and nonprofit actors (Newman 2001; Bakvis and Juillet 2004; Dunleavy et al. 2006; Osborne 2006). Finally, NPG also advocates a shift from economic to social and cultural values, based on participation and deliberation; public value search and production (Moore, 1995); and a new ethos of public service (Denhardt and Denhardt 2000). The centrality of "network governance" (Osborne 2006; 2010) derives from these shifts. Network governance is undoubtedly the backbone of NPG, although there are scholars in the field of public governance, such as Andresani and Ferlie (2006), who highlight how it represents an element of continuity between NPM and post-NPM reforms.[4]

Definitions and characterizations of NPG are numerous. In this section, as announced in the previous one, the argument about NPG will be developed by first referring to the formulation of its initiator, Osborne (2006, 2010); then presenting and discussing the definitions, as well as other relevant aspects, of the NPG's "twin" narrative, collaborative governance; finally, broadening the focus to include post-NPM doctrines, showing how they also aim to remedy the fragmentation caused by NPM, in fact, advancing a large part of the same solutions proposed by NPG (in its original formulation) and collaborative governance. The *fil rouge* of this excursus is represented by the focus on the state and, more generally, the public actor(s): Osborne (2006, 2010) proposes a precise representation of the state; collaborative governance, in line with its non-European but U.S. origins, is less inclined to think in terms of state (see Almond 1988) but raises the question of the role of the public actor(s) in collaborative networks; post-NPM doctrines explicitly aim at "reintegrating the fragmented state by focusing on government as a whole and joining up the parts through horizontal (and vertical) coordination" (Halligan 2010, 235).

For Osborne (2006, 384), NPG "posits both a plural state, where multiple inter-dependent actors contribute to the delivery of public services, and a pluralist state, where multiple processes inform the policy making system [...] its focus is very much upon inter-organizational relationships and the governance of processes, and it stresses service effectiveness and outcomes."

The conceptual sources underlying this formulation of NPG and the related representation of the state are multiple. As acknowledged by its initiator, the theoretical roots of NPG can be traced in the institutional theory (Osborne 2010, table 1.1, 11), the organizational sociology (Osborne 2006, table 1, 383), and the network theory (Osborne 2006, table 1, 383; 2010, table 1.1, 11). In addition to

---

[4] Because of this reason and other contradictions, Andresani and Ferlie (2006, abstract and 429) take a quite critical stance, inviting us to be skeptical of a network governance story as "purely horizontal-trustworthy-yet-to-come heaven-on-earth," which is the result of a self-reference paradox by public administration scholars.

these theoretical sources, the "political theories on active citizenship, empowerment, and participation" (Torfing and Triantafillou 2013, 12), as well as deliberation (Osborne and Strokosch 2022), are certainly another essential component. However, the eclectic (and therefore hybrid) inspiration of NPG does not stop there. As Liddle points out (2018, 970),

> Osborne extended Moore's ideas on public value (1995) and drew from several other strands of research on public management reform (Pollitt and Bouckaert 2011) pluralist approaches to network theory and New Public Services (NPS) (Denhart and Denhart 2000) to develop the approach of NPG (Osborne 2010). [. . .] It was also influenced by ideas on whole systems government (Benington and Hartley 2009) and the need for motivated and entrepreneurial public officials, as propounded also by think tanks.

Thus, Osborne is the entrepreneur of the NPG narrative, as he has combined already existing elements in a new way, so that innovation in NPG takes place via "recombination" instead of pure "invention" (Schumpeter 1934, 1947).

Moving on to the "twin" narrative, Ansell and Gash (2008, 544–545) define collaborative governance as "a governing arrangement where one or more public agencies directly engage non-state stakeholders in a collective decision-making process that is formal, consensus-oriented, and deliberative and that aims to make or implement public policy or manage public programs or assets." In this definition, requirements for formal-institutional context and public initiative are as essential as participatory-deliberative aspects. However, the idea of collaborative governance upheld by Emerson et al. (2012, 2) challenges these requirements by broadening the definition to include exclusively "private-social partnerships." Indeed, they define collaborative governance as "the processes and structures of public policy decision making and management that engage people constructively across the boundaries of public agencies, levels of government, and/or the public, private and civic spheres in order to carry out a public purpose that could not otherwise be accomplished."

These conflicting definitions shed light not only on the difficulties of drawing the boundaries of collaborative governance but also on the different roles assigned to the state or, better, public actors in network governance. This issue is important and deserves to be briefly discussed here by taking a stance on the existing debate. In the literature, the disputed points about the role of the public actor(s) in collaborative governance are mainly two: public initiative and the presence/absence of public institutions in collaborative networks. Concerning public initiative, it is convincing to embrace Emerson et al.'s (2012) position: it is collaborative governance even if the public actor has not activated the network and joins a preexisting network created by nongovernmental actors. The issue of the presence/absence of public institutions is more complex. A criterion for establishing which networks are "collaborative" from the perspective of collaborative governance can be found in the public dimension or not of the considered governance structures. Following this criterion, all (collaborative) networks are "collaborative governance structures," regardless of the presence or absence of public institutions, if: (1) they give (or try to give) answers to problems with collective relevance (i.e., perceived as public – Dunn 1981); (2) they produce outputs/outcomes that have a collective and potentially *erga omnes* value (performing a system political function, see Easton 1953 and Sartori 1973), as they are involved in the production of common/public goods, policies, and services. Finally, two further aspects deserve consideration: first, without these "requirements for publicness" (i.e., collective relevance of the problems and potentially *erga omnes* value), any entry of the public actor in a network would be implausible; second, the same entry of public institutions in a network most likely determines a formal interaction context among actors and organizations.

Beyond this specific dispute, what is important to underline is that, in fact, among the proponents of collaborative governance, not all would support what Klijn and Koppejan (2000, abstract) argue about network governance, namely, that "government's special resources and its unique legitimacy as representative of the common interest make it the outstanding candidate for fulfilling the role of network manager." Indeed, a significant stream of the collaborative governance narrative is inspired by an ethical ideal of substantial parity, even in terms of roles and contributions, between governmental and nongovernmental actors, that is, private for-profit and third-sector actors. This aspect differentiates especially "U.S." collaborative governance from "European" NPG, where the somewhat superordinated and impartial role of public administrations and the state is more preserved in the management and coordination of networks.

Reverting to the definitions of collaborative governance provided at the beginning, Emerson et al.'s definition (2012) highlights a crucial aspect: the need for cooperation as a basis for collaborative governance. Here, Barnard's lesson (1938) can be traced: collaborative governance fulfills the function of creating a coordinated organization, although a reticular one, able to achieve a goal that individual actors could not achieve alone.

The emphasis on collaboration and cooperation, along with the concern for coordination, is shared by both collaborative governance and NPG. However, the emphasis on these aspects, and especially collaboration, is more pronounced in the former than in the latter, as indicated by their respective designations or labels.

The attention to collaboration is so marked, particularly within collaborative governance, that it has influenced a conceptual systematization of cooperation, coordination, and collaboration, so to speak, "inverted." As McNamara (2012, 391) explains, "some theorists describe" these elements "as falling along a continuum of increased interaction": at one end of the continuum, cooperation; at the opposite end, collaboration; and, in the middle, coordination (see also O'Flynn 2009, 114–115). Along the continuum, interaction grows because collaboration would require "much closer relationships, connections, and resources and even a blurring of the boundaries between organizations" (Keast, Brown, and Mandell 2007, 19) compared to cooperation and coordination. Indeed, in cooperation, interaction would take place "within existing structures and policies, to serve individual interests" because the participants are capable of "to accomplish organizational goals, but chose to work together"; in coordination, it would consist of the mobilization of "formal linkages [. . .] because some assistance from others is needed to achieve organizational goals"; while, in collaboration, would take place "between participants who work together to pursue complex goals based on shared interests and a collective responsibility for interconnected tasks which cannot be accomplished individually" (McNamara 2012, 391). As anticipated, this kind of conceptual systematization is an interesting case of reassigning meanings with respect to both analytic and common languages. First, the three concepts hardly seem to be placeable on the same continuum. In analytical terms, cooperation and collaboration pertain to the "objectives" dimension, while coordination pertains to the "means" dimension, as evidenced by the definition of coordination as an "instrumental process" (Keast, Brown and Mandell 2007, 18). Second, even in common language and meanings, collaborating, despite the alleged etymological reconstructions, is usually less than cooperating and not vice versa: cooperation is generally oriented to achieve "big" common objectives that necessarily require a certain alignment of interests, while collaboration is oriented toward more specific and, so to speak, "medium and small range" objectives and tasks. Clearly, this reassignment of meanings is not unrelated to the spread and success of the collaborative governance narrative; on the contrary, it is functional to reinforce the "mythic aura" and the "cult of collaboration" (O'Flynn 2009) as a governance solution.

Moving beyond the focus on collaborative governance, the central elements of cooperation, collaboration, and coordination are also strongly present in other discourses, which assume different names according to the geographic reference. In addition to the U.S. collaborative governance (Agranoff 2006; Bryson et al. 2006; Kettl 2006; McGuire 2006; Thomson and Perry 2006), there are also narratives that are generally defined as "post-NPM" doctrines: *joined-up government* as it developed in the U.K. and New Zealand (Pollitt 2003; Bogdanor 2005; Gregory 2003), Australia's *whole-of-government* (Halligan 2006; Christensen and Lægreid 2007a); and Canada's *horizontal management* (Bakvis and Juillet 2004).

In response to public administration fragmentation and "pillarization" (Pollitt 2003; Gregory 2003) caused by managerial reforms, the imperatives of the post-NPM, intended as a "more holistic strategy using insights from the other social sciences rather than just economics" (Christensen and Lægreid 2007a, 1059), are two: "coordination" and "integration" (Christensen 2012; Mulgan 2005).

In NPG, as an umbrella term that also includes the post-NPM doctrines, coordination becomes a "focal issue" because "working across organizational, jurisdictional and political/administrative boundaries will enable more efficient and/or effective policy development and implementation and service delivery" (Christensen 2012, 2). Post-NPM has remedied the coordination issue through "the reassertion of the center" (Halligan 2006), that is, re-centralization: "the core ideas of post-NPM are to strengthen the central political order through structural reintegration and by increasing capacity at the top" (Christensen and Fan 2016, 4). In this respect, post-NPM reforms seem to implement a strategy that contrasts NPM's "deconcentration of power" (Aucoin 1990): centralization, coordination, and integration challenge decentralization, deregulation, and delegation. In the words of Lapuente and Van de Walle (2020, 463), "post-NPM represents a reassertion of old public administration values as well an attempt to remedy some of the disintegrating tendencies associated with NPM, and not an abandonment of NPM reforms." In particular, post-NPM "complements the specialization, fragmentation, and marketization characteristic of NPM reforms with more coordination, centralization and collaborative capacity." For these reasons, the authors conclude that "one should talk more of continuity rather than a clear break between NPM and post-NPM reforms."

Part of the post-NPM integration strategy is the insistence on collective cultural norms and values (Christensen and Fan 2016, 4), and the need to "reestablish a 'common ethic' and a 'cohesive culture' in the public sector because of reported corrosion of loyalty and increasing distrust" by citizens toward institutions (Christensen and Lægreid 2007a, 1062). For this reason, it is also necessary to develop a new ethos of public service (Denhardt and Denhardt 2000; Stoker 2006) through the drafting of new guidelines and codes of ethics, able to keep the various public agencies united under the slogan "we need to work together" (Christensen and Lægreid 2007a, 1062), "stressing that people are in the 'same cultural boat' since they have a common cultural heritage and a common future" (Christensen and Fan 2016, 4). Of course, the insistence on collective cultural norms and shared values is also a crucial part of NPG, which promotes a plural and pluralist vision of the state (Osborne 2006; 2010), as well as in collaborative governance. Values and principles of action oriented toward the "creation of individual and societal value" (Osborne and Strokosch 2022), such as "participation," "deliberation," "coproduction" (see inter al. Bovaird

2007; Pestoff 2006; 2012), and "cocreation," highlight the attention paid to legitimacy and institutional trust: the goal is the (complementary) strengthening of democratic and representative institutions.

Much has been written about participation and coproduction; hence, these aspects will not be addressed here. Instead, it is worth briefly focusing on cocreation, considering the growing significance it is gaining within NPG. Ansell and Torfing (2021, 6) define cocreation as "the process through which a broad range of interdependent actors engage in distributed, cross-boundary collaboration in order to define common problems and design and implement new and better solutions." According to the authors, it "could become the backbone" of NPG, even being understood as a "new public governance paradigm," since it would provide "an attractive and feasible alternative to the false choice between Weberian bureaucracies based on hierarchical command and control, NPM reforms that run the public sector like a private business, and communitarian dreams of a society based on democratic self-government in small enclosed communities sheltered from the systemic power of the state and the market economy" (Ansell and Torfing 2021, 4 and 2).

Within the framework of NPG's "cohesive strategy," which is founded on the principles of participation, deliberation, coproduction, and cocreation, leadership plays a fundamental role. In NPG, leadership is intended as public leadership, concerning three spheres: political, administrative, and civic leadership (Hart and Uhr 2008). Therefore, leaders can be not only politicians or public managers but also civil society actors belonging to the nongovernmental sectors, both profit and nonprofit. In the NPG narrative, leadership is essentially transformational (Bass, 1985; Burns, 1978), since leaders are represented as agents of change and social innovators (see Torfing and Ansell 2017; de Vries et al. 2018). Several labels are associated with leadership in NPG (Van Wart 2013; Sørensen and Torfing 2015): "facilitative" (Svara 1994), "horizontal" (Denis et al. 2012), "cohesive," "community," "ethical" and "public value" (Getha-Taylor 2009), and – above all – "collaborative" and "integrative" leadership (Bono et al. 2010; Crosby and Bryson 2010; Morse 2007, 2010; Ospina and Foldy 2010; Page 2010). NPG leaders should be "metagovernors" (Sørensen 2006) and "facilitators of the democratic process being especially sensitive to the needs to foster civic networks, public dialogue, and voice for the disenfranchised" (Van Wart 2013, 522).[5] Indeed, as Torfing and Triantafillou (2013, 20–21) point out, "NPG is increasingly defined as a third order activity

---

[5] Although integrative leadership is recognized as a key factor in NPG settings, Crosby and Bryson (2010, 227) suggest not overestimate its impact, insisting that "the normal expectation ought to be that success will be very difficult to achieve in cross-sector collaborations, regardless of leadership effectiveness."

involving the governance of governance arenas," that is, "metagovernance," intended as "a reflexive, strategic, and inherently political mode of governance that aims to sponsor and frame interactive policy processes, bring actors together, facilitate collaboration, mediate conflict, support decision making, and ensure implementation of negotiated solutions."

Moving toward the end of this section, it becomes valuable to make some remarks about the "triggering factors" and driving forces behind the emergence of NPG, as well as its diffusion and success. Concerning the emergence of NPG, they are, like in every new governance narrative, essentially two: first, the "functional" need to respond to societal and socio-technical change that gives rise to new demands, needs, but also opportunities. Second, a corrective and learning dynamic connected to the critique of previous ideational constructs and their implementation (see Torfing et al. 2020, 16; Pollitt and Bouckaert 2004). Instead, the development and success of a governance narrative depend on the diffusion of new governance ideas across organizations, sectors, and countries. Diffusion is, to a large extent, connected to isomorphic mechanisms (DiMaggio and Powell 1983): certainly the mimetic ones, especially where the environment is characterized by uncertainty; but also the coercive ones, connected to the need to respond to common external challenges and, more generally, to binding contexts of action; and normative mechanisms, based on – more or less mythical (Meyer and Rowan 1977) – beliefs of governance as a "cognitive base" actively conveyed by specific "professional groups" such as academics and practitioners.

Behind NPG, the relevance of the second driver is quite evident: since the beginning, NPG, such as an "emergent" and "new model" (Halligan 2007), has been presented, and, to a large extent, continues to be coconstructed, as an NPM counternarrative. In this regard, a point that needs to be underlined right from here is that NPG's chances of success in terms of diffusion seem to depend more on the legitimacy that derives from its perhaps mythical "otherness" compared to the "dominant paradigm," that is, NPM, rather than on the governance capacity linked to the offer of new solutions and tools. In fact, this section has highlighted how, in NPG, most of the proposed solutions are situated at the level of principles, such as participation, deliberation, and cocreation of public value, rather than being concrete tools.

The core elements that are the basis of the (co)construction of NPG as a counternarrative stand out in Table 1, which summarizes and compares some fundamental aspects of the three narratives of the contemporary adminis-tration: TPA, NPM, and NPG. The table was built on the basis of Osborne (2006, table 1, 383; 2010, table 1.1, 11) and Wiesel and Modell (2014), but it was integrated with other elements derived from literature on leadership, professionalism, accountability (Goodin 2003), types of governance

Table 1 Core elements of NPG compared to TPA and NPM

ELEMENTS	TPA	NPM	NPG
Theoretical roots	political science public policy public administration	managerialism public choice	institutional sociology organizational sociology network theory political theories on active citizenship, participation, and deliberation
Nature of the state	unitary	divisionalized (disaggregated – Osborne 2006)	plural and pluralist
Structures and forms of organizing	unitary bureaucracies	(quasi) competitive markets	collaborative networks
Focus	policy system	intra-organizational management	interorganizational governance
Tasks of agencies	policy execution	market exchange	network coordination
Types of governance	procedural governance	corporate and market governance	network governance
Governance mechanisms	hierarchy	market and contracts	trust or relational contracts
Mechanisms of accountability	hierarchy	competition	cooperative networks (multiple forms of accountability)
Main focuses of control	inputs and intra-organizational processes	outputs	interorganizational processes and outcomes

Key performance aspects	compliance with rules and regulations	efficiency customer satisfaction	effectiveness citizen satisfaction
Core values	public sector ethos professionalism	competition managerialism	collaboration cooperation integration participation coproduction and cocreation public value new ethos of public service new professionalism
Conceptions of public employees	Weberian servants	rational individual utility maximizers	both state-agents and citizen-agents, selfish and altruistic motivations (mixed-motives view)
Approaches to public service ethos	monopoly by the PA	skeptical of public sector ethos	diffused public service ethos shared values
Leadership	political leadership	administrative leadership transactional leadership entrepreneurial leadership	public leadership (also civic) transformational leadership facilitative, collaborative, ethical, public value leadership
Conceptions of citizens	constituents/ taxpayers	customers/consumers	coproducers

Table 1 (cont.)

ELEMENTS	TPA	NPM	NPG
Public–private relations	functional separation (but public dominance via public regulation of markets)	public *vs.* private as competition for more (public) efficiency (deregulation and private dominance)	public *plus* private (i.e., for-profit AND nonprofit/third sector) as synergy
Field-level logics	bureaucracy	market-capitalism	democracy

Source: Table elaborated by the author, revisited from Osborne (2006, 2010) and Wiesel and Modell (2014) plus, inter al., Considine and Lewis (2003), Goodin (2003), Polzer et al. (2016), Stoker (2006), Torfing and Triantafillou (2013).

(Considine and Lewis 2003), and ethos of public service (Stoker 2006). Other sources are Polzer et al. (2016), Torfing and Triantafillou (2013),[6] and Maynard-Moody and Musheno (2000 – about state- and citizen-agents).

5 NPG as a Hybrid

This section delves into the debate on the relationship between NPG and NPM and the argument of NPG as a hybrid. Firstly, it explicitly presents the thesis of this contribution. Then, it introduces the two major hypotheses in the literature: the "linear substitution" hypothesis and the "continuity and hybridization" one, along with their respective supporters. Finally, it presents a series of arguments in favor of the second hypothesis, highlighting sources of continuity and hybridization elements, understood as "old (and sometimes contrasting) elements" that make NPG a hybrid (see Introduction). So, among sources of continuity are public choice, the theory of governance, and consumerism, while among hybridization elements are interorganizational approach, polycentricity, coproduction, market, networks, hierarchy, and so on.

Although NPG has a reactive *origin* to NPM (as it emerged as a response to the failures of the adversarial and managerial modes of policy making and implementation – Ansell and Gash 2008), this contribution argues that its oppositive *nature* (i.e., its irreconcilability with NPM's fundamental tenets and ideas) has been rhetorically overemphasized: NPG has been and is still often presented as a governance counternarrative and a radical alternative to NPM, in order to gain a sort of competitive advantage in terms of legitimacy over the (until then) dominant narrative, that is, NPM, which, although "is by no means over," has undoubtedly been "challenged" (Christensen and Lægreid 2007b, 1) because of its shortcomings and unintended consequences. In fact, as Dickinson noted (2016, 45), "while there has been extensive rhetoric concerning governance shifts, the reality is that rather than seeing wholesale shifts we are faced instead with overlapping layers of different reform [narratives and] processes."

In the debate on NPG and NPM (but also TPA), about their relationship and nature, two different hypotheses relating to the development of new governance models or paradigms are central: the "linear substitution" hypothesis and the "continuity and hybridization" one.

---

[6] Torfing and Triantafillou (2013) propose an NPG analysis based on David Easton's system theoretical model. They also develop a table (Figure 2, 14) in which they compare TPA (for them, Classical Public Administration), NPM, and NPG according to the analytical categories of input, withinput, output, and feedback. This framework offers a perspective, if not directly integrable, complementary and largely compatible with the one adopted here.

Regarding the former, several authors believe that a new governance model is supplanting NPM by virtue of its complete "otherness" in terms of values and actions. Actually, this idea also finds support in a literal interpretation of Osborne's provocation (2006, 377): here, NPG is presented as the third, new, stage after TPA and NPM. Certainly, among them, there are Denhardt and Denhardt (2000, 557), who write:

> From a theoretical perspective, the New Public Service offers an important and viable alternative to both the traditional and the now-dominant managerialist models. [. . .] The result is a normative model, comparable to other such models. [. . .] If we assume the responsibility of government is to facilitate individual self-interest, we will take one set of action. If, on the other hand, we assume the responsibility of government is to promote citizenship, public discourse, and the public interest, we will take an entirely different set of action.

Entwistle and Martin (2005, 233) are also attributable to this hypothesis as they argue in favor of an actual collaborative "turn" after the era of competition promoted by Thatcher and Major. Finally, Dunleavy et al. (2006, 468) even state that "the intellectually and practically dominant set of managerial and governance ideas of the last two decades, new public management (NPM), has essentially died in the water [. . .] key parts of the NPM reform message have been reversed because they lead to policy disasters, and other large parts are stalled." Thus, the linear substitution hypothesis implies a quite radical change, if not a subversion of the previous governance model.

On the opposite side, the "continuity and hybridization" hypothesis was formulated by Wiesel and Modell (2014, 177 and 180) in terms of "the process through which elements of diverse governance logics are integrated into context-specific configurations of governance practices." Within this framework, the transition from one governance logic to another is only partial and takes place through "the retention of key elements of extant logics in emerging configurations." Among others, also Koppenjan and Koliba (2013, 2) are largely in line with this hypothesis as they comment: "it is far from clear that emergent forms of governance will replace existing arrangements. Rather, it may be hypothesized that they will mix with bureaucracy and new public management arrangements, thus resulting in hybrid forms of governance" (see also Koliba et al. 2010; Koppenjan 2012; about post-NPM, see Christensen 2012, 7).

Now that the two main hypotheses present in the literature have been explained, it is possible to proceed with presenting the arguments in favor of the "continuity and hybridization" hypothesis and the NPG as a hybrid.

The first argument highlights how several constitutive elements of NPG, such as the interorganizational approach, polycentricity, and coproduction, can be traced back not to NPM *tout court*, but to one of the two main theoretical components underlying NPM, namely new institutional economics, and more specifically, public choice.

Indeed, in the literature, it is widely recognized that NPM is a complex doctrinal puzzle and the result of "a marriage of opposites" (Hood 1991, 5) that correspond to those indicated by Aucoin (1990): managerialism (rooted in classical organization theories and scientific management principles – Pollitt 1990), and new institutional economics (a broader label that includes public choice, transaction costs economics, and principal–agent theory).[7] In fact, new institutional economics has a bottom-up and progressive soul, certainly more than a managerialism that can be interpreted as "top-down" and, even, neo Taylorism (Pollitt 1990; see Cataldi 2017; Cataldi and Tousijn 2015).

Thus, it is not surprising that NPG's criticism is directed primarily at one of the two main theoretical components underlying NPM, namely its most hierarchical, top-down, and conservative stream, that is, managerialism, and that, conversely, the other stream, that is, new institutional economics, and specifically public choice, is a source of continuity and hybridization elements.

In particular, two important pieces of the NPG's theoretical construction can be found in the public choice: interorganizational approach and coproduction.

With reference to the former, Osborne (2006, 383 – table 1) argues that the primary focus of NPG is "inter-organizational governance" *versus* NPM's "intra-organizational management." However, he acknowledges that "Ostrom and Ostrom (1971) offer a more explicitly inter-organizational approach to public choice theory as a basis for the NPM" (Osborne 2006, note 4, 385), admitting, in fact, an important element of continuity between NPG and NPM. Actually, the (indirect) contribution of the Ostroms and colleagues to NPG is not limited to the interorganizational perspective but includes their theory of polycentricity (Ostrom 2005; Ostrom et al. 1961). In their studies on metropolitan areas, the Ostroms highlight the existence of a "mixed economy with substantial private participation in the delivery of public services" (Ostrom and Ostrom [1977] 1999, 76), that is, of "a public-private industry rather than with the bureaucratic apparatus of a single government" (Ostrom 1996, 1079).

---

[7] The theoretical roots of NPM are also multiple. Although the main streams are two, the inspirational sources are not limited to managerialism and new institutional economics, since, as Gruening (2001, 8) argues, they include a variety of ideas and theoretical perspectives, such as classical and neoclassical public administration, policy analysis, property-rights theory, the neo-Austrian school, and New Public Administration. Therefore, also "NPM is a mixture [i.e. a hybrid] of values" (Bojang 2020, 5).

The variety of relationships between governmental units, public agencies, and private businesses "can be coordinated through [different] patterns of interorganizational arrangements:" not only coordination by "bureaucratic command structures" but also "self-regulating tendencies" and mechanisms (Ostrom and Ostrom 1965, 135–136). The result is the conceptualization of metropolitan areas in terms of "polycentric political system as having many centers of decision making that were formally independent of each other" (Ostrom 1972 in McGinnis 1999, 53). Thus, not only the interorganizational perspective but also the idea of a polycentric governance system is a core conceptual legacy in NPG.

With reference to the latter, that is, coproduction, Wiesel and Modell (2014, 179) affirm that "NPG logic represents a transition towards growing recognition of the wider and more pro-active involvement of citizens as co-producers in more collaborative systems of public service provision" (see also Sorrentino et al. 2018). The concept of coproduction has clearly identifiable origins in public choice (Ostrom 1996, 1078–1079). In one of its first formulations, public services "coproduction involves a mixing of the productive efforts of regular and consumer producers" (Parks et al. 1981, 1002). But, over time, it has progressively extended from the production of public services to public policies and governance (see Cataldi 2015).

In conclusion, interorganizational approach (as well as polycentricity) and coproduction are not only key to public choice but are also NPG's milestones.

Besides interorganizational approach, polycentricity, and coproduction, there are further reasons why it is not possible to agree with the hypothesis of "a linear development whereby the notion of NPG largely replaces some previously entrenched NPM logic" (Wiesel and Modell 2014, 180).

The second argument in favor of the "continuity and hybridization" hypothesis identifies the theory of governance, as the wider "discursive object" from which NPG descends, as an important vehicle for hybridization and a source of continuity. Indeed, in order to understand NPG – as well as collaborative governance or other labels – it is necessary to revisit the theory of governance. Although the latter has a much larger semantic domain than NPG, it is impossible to leave it aside when discussing "modern governance" (Kooiman 1993). As Pierre and Peters (2000) point out, opposite concepts are traceable in the theory of governance: not only "good governance" and "governance as a community," but "market," "NPM," and "government" ("governance as hierarchy"). The "dualistic" representation of governance, as opposed to government, has been challenged by numerous scholars (Whitehead 2003). Pierre and Peters (2000) suggested that the state still plays a leading role in governance processes, although governance relates to changing relationships between state and society, as well as a growing reliance on less coercive policy instruments. Moreover, according to the theory of metagovernance (see Jessop 2002; Kooiman 2003; Sørensen 2006; Torfing et al. 2012), governance would be the result of three ways of organizing society: state, market, and networks (Keast et al. 2006). On this basis, it becomes evident that the theory of governance (i.e., the 'object' behind NPG, from which it descends) is itself a hybrid. Indeed, governance not only takes shape "in the shadow of hierarchy" (Scharpf 1994) but reiterates the indispensability of government: public institutions (and elected politicians) have the role of governing "crowded" policy arenas and choosing the right mix of state, market, and networks (Keast et al. 2006; see also Torfing et al. 2012, 123 and 235).

The third argument identifies as a further element of hybridization precisely the (persistence of) the market and, more specifically, the substantial acceptance by NPG of the market logics as a mode of regulation of the society and public sector. In fact, in NPG, beyond the proclamations about the necessity to de-marketize the public sector, the market does not disappear but remains both as a real practice and in the "cognitive horizon" of the NPG advocates themselves. As claimed by Fattore et al. (2012, 219), "new governance' ideals are constructed both from supposed virtues of markets and third sector alternatives to the state, as well as from the belief in the virtue of competition, choice, and multi-agent collaboration." What has been said reveals a trait of continuity that goes beyond real governance practices, which are inevitably more tangled than theory, involving precisely the ideational assumptions: in NPG as a rhetorical discourse, the existence of the market is not heralded but is somehow justified inside plural arenas. Ultimately, the market is an unavoidable piece of the (liberal)democratic, plural and pluralist construction of NPG. Yet NPG seems to have a theoretical debt also to the Third way (see Osborne 2010, 23) "which supports a 'mixed economy' within the public sector and seeks 'a synergy between public and private sectors, utilizing the dynamism of markets but with the public interest in mind' (Giddens 1998, 78, 100)" (Considine and Lewis 2003, 132), thus combining competitive market with state and "economic innovation with social justice" (Benington 2011, 41).

The fourth argument is that another element of continuity and hybridization is represented by consumerism, which has expanded, and even widened, in the shift from NPM to NPG (Powell et al. 2010). While, in NPM, the power of user choice was connected to the creation of a competitive (or quasi) market, in NPG, it "does not necessarily require the existence of market-like arrangements," although the market persists, and it is functional to ensure better embeddedness of consumerist notions (Wiesel and Modell 2014, 176).

Finally, after concluding the arguments centered around identifying sources of continuity for and hybridization elements within NPG, an additional argument in favor of the "continuity and hybridization" hypothesis concerns the label "post-NPM." In this contribution, this label properly refers to doctrines such as "joined-up government" and "whole-of-government" that have been included under the broad umbrella of NPG, but clearly, as often occurs in the literature, it can be extended to NPG as an umbrella term. The argument is that the label "post-NPM" itself contradicts the hypothesis of a linear substitution (and a radical transition) from NPM to NPG. Indeed, it tends to underline both continuity, as it involves a substantial admission that it is not possible to define the present without referencing the past, represented by NPM, and the presence of hybridization elements. For instance, Christensen and Fan (2016, 4) state to use the term "post-NPM" precisely because it combines hierarchical structural and horizontal integrative elements.

The arguments developed in this section suggest that different governance elements often overlap, juxtapose, or develop in tandem without replacing altogether (see Andresani and Ferlie 2006; Hood and Peters 2004) and that NPG's hybridity, intended as a coexistence of different institutional – and discursive – logics (Goodrick and Reay 2011), takes the specific form of "layering and sedimentation" (Mahoney and Thelen 2010; Streeck and Thelen 2005; about post-NPM see also Christensen and Fan 2016). Polzer et al. (2016) argue that this type of hybridity differs from both "transitional combinations," eventually leading to the replacement, and "blending" as an "indiscernible amalgamated." Conversely, Torfing et al. (2020, 3) assert that "the competing and co-existing governance paradigms will both form a layer cake with relatively separate public governance regimes and a marble cake with mixed and hybrid forms of public governance." Actually, "layers" can collapse, especially in the absence of dowel rods placed by a clever pastry chef (the state or government, and, more generally, public administrations/institutions?). Thus, "despite hybridity being a relatively well-established concept in the literature," what is missing is "how to navigate the complexities that this produces" (Dickinson 2016, 55) and how to govern hybrid governance (Crouch 2005). On this front, issues about the state or government, and, more generally, public administrations/institutions, such as their representations, roles and legitimacy, as well as their governance capacity, are fundamental pieces of the puzzle.

6 Reasons for NPG Hybridization

The previous section presented arguments that support the "continuity and hybridization" hypothesis and, more generally, NPG as a hybrid, focusing on the identification of sources of continuity and hybridization elements. Instead, this one addresses the reasons for hybridization. Therefore, it answers the question: what has favored, and continues to favor, the hybridization process of NPG with NPM?

The reasons for hybridization pivot on four arguments, labelled "structural compatibility," "continuity," "inspiration from the 'private'," and "lack of an effective opposition." These labels do not claim to adequately summarize the arguments developed herein but serve the purpose of facilitating the reading of this section.

The first reason for the hybridization of NPG with NPM can be found in the so-called "structural compatibility." According to this hypothesis, NPM and NPG have different focuses: NPM deals with the interior of the bureaucratic organization, while NPG with its exterior, that is, the relations with the environment. In this sense, the interlocking of the two would seem to be easy. In fact, however, it is more complicated, and there are areas of overlap: the contrast between internal vs. external focus is attenuated as, for instance, NPM recommends contracting out (i.e., outsourcing) and NPG advocates trust-based management (see also Table 1, row "Governance mechanisms"). Yet, complementarity is explicitly sought at the narrative level, albeit insisting on a different value framework: "NPG was argued to rectify the often narrow intraorganizational focus of NPM (Osborne 2006, 2010) by conceptualizing a public governance system as extending beyond the immediate contract to the external environment, encompassing exchanges between individuals and/or groups and/or organizations" (Mills et al. 2021, 502).

The second reason focuses precisely on continuity. Thus, the "continuity" reason references and, so to speak, summarizes the previous section, reinterpreting (and expanding) it in terms of reasons for hybridization. The core argument is that NPG has largely structured itself for intentional differentiation from NPM, but NPG and NPM have a history and key points in common. The history of both is TPA, but also the theory of governance and public choice. Therefore, one of the reasons that have favored and continue to favor the hybridization of NPG with NPM can be attributed exactly to this shared history and theoretical elaborations.

The third reason pertains to the "inspiration from the 'private'" argument. It highlights how an element that favors the hybridization of NPG with NPM is that both draw inspiration from "the private" (intended as "other than the state" and "other than the public") for the management, governance, and reform of the public sector, albeit with significant differences. Indeed, NPM is inspired by market organizations, while NPG is primarily inspired by the relational dynamics (and network structures) of civil society (especially the third sector). The shared belief – or, perhaps, a belief borrowed from NPM by NPG – that importing ideas and best practices from the "private world" can successfully enhance the public sector, in fact, paves the way for the hybridization of NPG with NPM. The evidence lies in the role of multiple actors both from the private (i.e., "for-profit") and third sectors, which NPG underscores in the plural arenas meant to invigorate the public sector.

More generally, this belief continues to fuel an effective hybridization of the public sector, even in the era of the emerging NPG narrative. It is appropriate, then, to clarify aspects of the public sector hybridization process that hold relevance even for NPG, as they provide significant general insights. In the public sector, hybridization is certainly structural since there is no longer only the state-bureaucracy, intended as a cohesive hierarchical structure of authority, but the same state-organization includes market and network forms (Powell 1990). However, hybridization also occurs between different logics, criteria of accountability (Goodin 2003), and different forms of rationality (e.g., legal-rational and economic rationalities). Thus, the public sector's hybridization process consists precisely of the multidimensional and persistent blurring "with other sectors and more social actors" (Denis et al. 2015, abstract; see also Benn and Gaus 1983; Wise 2010). Here, the term "persistent" refers to the fact that public policies and services have always been realized through implementation structures (Hjern and Porter 1981) characterized by a mix of state, private (i.e., for profit), and third sector, as well as more informal and private elements of the civil society (Ostrom 1996). Following this line of argument, the involvement of nongovernmental organizations (for profit or not) in the production of public services can certainly be an example of hybridization (Wise 2010). However, it is a known phenomenon that can be considered "new" only in terms of its extent, modalities, and historical contingencies. Furthermore, hybridization does not solely concern the implementation structures but the organizations themselves, which can be conceived as positioned along a continuum of "publicness-privateness" (Moulton 2009; Wise 2010).

The fourth and final reason for hybridization refers to the "lack of an effective opposition" argument. At its core, it highlights that, although "many academics and even government officials are proclaiming that the NPM is dead" (Lindquist 2009, 44), including Dunleavy et al. (2006) and the Danish Social Democratic Prime Minister, Mette Frederiksen, actually, among political-administrative élites, there are no effective opponents to the (pragmatic) combination between NPM and NPG. An explanation of this "lack of an effective opposition" is that, as Eymeri-Douzans (2013, 504-505) argued about France and other "NPM-laggards," "NPM is a very ductile product," thanks to the strength of its "second nature," the praxeological one, defined as "a toolkit" and "a practical repertoire of recipes and techniques." Indeed, the neo-managerialist "praxeologic" not only supports but has the ability to transcend the ideological dimension of NPM, intended as "a discourse which promotes a system of 'core beliefs' and value-oriented precepts about what the state and its administrations ought to be, beliefs and precepts well in line with the dominant neo-liberal *Zeitgeist* of the three latest decades." That's why the "'praxeological' dimension of NPM appears to be its major driver of diffusion: those in power in the state structure, both the elected governors and the administrative elite, can import the neo-managerial toolkit without having to declare explicitly their adhesion to [or even publicly opposing] the founding ideological corpus of NPM."

Finally, alongside these four reasons, it is worth highlighting that the hybridization process finds support in the "avoidance of blame" mechanism illustrated by Christensen and Lægreid (2006, 7) in post-NPM: the *pendulum* of the reform, which swings between devolution and "reassertion of the center," is also motivated by the administrators' attempt to avoid blame "when things go wrong," sometimes resorting to delegation (Aucoin 1990) and sometimes firmly keeping in their hands power, influence, and information. As Dunelavy et al. (2006, 489) comment, "zigzag government policies – broader switches to and from decentralization/centralization or agencification/reintegration – can also be cynically interpreted as inevitable cycles."

7 Reasons for NPM Persistence/Dominance

In addition to the reasons for hybridization, it is then necessary to explore the motivations for NPM's persistence and dominance. Thus, the section represents a sort of answer to the question raised by Hyndman and Liguori (2016, 28): why are NPM ideas so pervasive in discussions and debates surrounding public administration?

The structure of the session is as follows. First, the issue of NPM persistence/dominance in the literature is presented. Afterward, the reasons for the persistence/dominance of NPM are illustrated. They pivot on four arguments: "toolkit and TPA anchoring," "legs," "common knowledge," and "shortcomings' compensation/reduction." The same disclaimer as the previous session applies to these labels.

In the literature, several scholars have addressed the issue of NPM persistence. Indeed, the emergence of a new narrative "does not mean that NPM has disappeared" (Fattore et al. 2012, 219). On the contrary, "it remains relatively important and has merged with and been partly modified by post-NPM" (Christensen and Fan 2016, 2). As stated by Fattore et al. (2012, 219), although the interest in NPM-inspired management tools is being challenged more than before, "it has not evaporated and is likely to remain." de Vries (2010, 4 and 3) argues that "though the NPM paradigm is in trouble, it is still far too early to speak in terms of a third-order [i.e., paradigmatic] change," concluding that "NPM is not really dead: parts of it are still very much alive." With reference to the CEE countries, Randma-Liiv and Drechsler (2017, 601) observe that "although the NPM model was basically deemed obsolete [. . .], it resurfaced to some extent and in some countries in 2008–2012 because of the global financial crisis (NPM as a toolbox never really went away, although the legitimacy of the tools was less questioned during theoretical NPM dominance and more so after its wane)." The authors then comment on the appearance of the new governance narratives in this way:

> with the NWS, other [. . .] "paradigmettes" (because they exist in parallel to each other, with none rising to real dominance), arose, [. . .] which wanted to preserve the basic NPM idea but now entailed lessons learned [. . .]. These include, first of all, NPG[8] as, basically, NPM with Weberian lessons learned, and with a public policy rather than an implementation focus (i.e., the mirror image of the NWS), but also coordination-emphasizing JUG and WoG.

Some other scholars have even posited that "NPM doctrine is also getting stronger" (Hajnal and Rosta 2015, 9), thus supporting not just the NPM's persistence thesis, but also the NPM's current and future dominance one: "NPM tools and techniques will grow in importance of the next period of public service management" (Kinder 2012, 422). Among these scholars, there are Massey (2019) and Hammerschmid et al. (2019). The former claims that "although some observers have argued the 'death' of NPM has occurred (Dunleavy et al. 2006), the NPM approach continues to dominate official methods to public sector reform, even after the [financial] crisis has passed. NPM then represents a meme; indeed, more an egregore producing mimetic isomorphism in the guise of policy learning and transfer taking place" (Massey 2019, 14–15)." The latter asserts that "NPM-inspired reforms have dominated public sector agendas in Europe for most of the 1990s and 2000s, and still do in many countries even though new reform paradigms have emerged" (Hammerschmid et al. 2019, 400).

The first reason for NPM's persistence hinges on the "toolkit and TPA anchoring" argument. It is based on the theory that "a pronounced element of hybridization is necessary [. . .] to penetrate the operating core of public sector

---

[8] About CEE countries, Reinholde et al. (2020, 12) write: "NPG is becoming the most wanted and admired public administration model nowadays, which is directed against NPM shortages with its qualities of openness, transparency, democracy, pluralism, social responsibility, social justice, social quality, anti-corruption and more active non-governmental organizations. Despite its theoretical attractiveness, however, NPG is still lacking the concrete methods of implementation."

organizations" (Wiesel and Modell 2014, 199). This theory clearly alludes to what has been previously mentioned in this Element: NPG seems to propose models of management, governance, and reform that are too abstract, and ultimately lacking in terms of concrete administrative tools. In this respect, hybridization with NPM, as a praxeological doctrine largely in line with the hierarchical-bureaucratic precepts of TPA, represents an entry point for NPG in public administrations. More explicitly, the persistence of NPM is motivated by two concrete administrative "virtues," both of which are actually attributable to the managerial stream: its provision of, and ultimately its being, "a toolkit," and its strong anchoring to TPA.

The second reason refers to the "legs" argument. It maintains that the NPM narrative – unlike NPG, which requires "metagovernors" (Sørensen 2006) and facilitative, integrative, and collaborative leaders able to operate "in cross-sector regimes" (Crosby and Bryson 2005), which are difficult to find and to educate – has strong internal legs to walk: managers of public bureaucracies. This argument is reinforced by Morse's observation (2007, 13), where he emphasizes that "In an age of collaborative governance, [...] the public leader must truly become the kind of person with whom others can trust and respect. [...] skills or tools will be useless if the personal attributes are not in alignment. The attributes must come first." Precisely these personal attributes, that so much remember the great man theory of leadership (Van Wart 2003), are the hard thing to find. However, it is necessary to remember here that the idea of metagovernance is not attributable only to NPG and the other "new" network governance narratives, such as collaborative/interactive governance. Indeed, Torfing et al. (2012, 122–123) recognize a "metagovernance *avant la lettre*" in NPM. Furthermore, in the "more managerial perspective" of Klijn and Koppenjan (2004) it is up to public managers to be metagovernors: they have to "manage complex networks in order to facilitate mutual learning and trust building" (Sørensen and Torfing 2009, 245). Thus, the challenge of metagovernance and metagovernors is to some extent common to both NPG and NPM, but the latter has the (persistent) advantage of "internal legs" to walk upon.

The third reason is based on the "common knowledge" argument. More precisely, it refers to the supposed superiority of NPM as "common knowledge" (Bozeman, 1993), both in public administration and academia. The concept of "common knowledge" recalls not a higher level of structuring of NPM as a "core set of ideas"[9] but the role of "*managerialese*" as "the Latin of our

---

[9] NPM and NPG/post-NPM are both "shopping bags" or "baskets" (inter al. Christensen 2012, 1; Pollitt 1995, 133; Pollitt and Bouckhaert 2011, 219; Van de Walle and Hammerschmid 2011, 191), although the assortment of elements is quite different (Klenk and Reiter 2019, 4). Thus, the NPM "higher structuring" is more correctly a higher level of "coding" and "categorization" of

days"[10] and "global vocabulary of administration" (Gherardi and Jacobsson 2000, 354). Following the "mythical perspective" (Christensen and Lægreid 2007a), NPM would have become for the contemporary public administration a rationalized myth (Meyer and Rowan, 1977), that is, a (dominant) "medium of codification and legitimation," so that "it has become difficult if not impossible for public organizations that want to be considered as modern, not to include these ideas in their own vocabulary and presentations" (Gherardi and Jacobsson 2000, 349–350).

With reference to the myths' functions, Goldfinch and Wallis (2010, 1099) observe:

> myth is not something simply "untrue", an unexamined doctrine that will fall away in the face of rational thought and empirical evidence. It has an existence and function above and beyond an empirical "reality". It can serve vital political and ideological functions, suppress and mediate conflict by providing unifying symbols, language and understandings, and harness emotional and intellectual energy towards political and policy reform ends. It gives a simplifying, familiar, and emotionally comforting structure, and an apparent understanding, to a complex, confusing, and barely understood policy world. Myth is the sometimes unstated and taken-for-granted "common sense" of a policy community and as such, once established, is resistant to challenge.

Ultimately, myth has a legitimation function since it defines what is acceptable and "appropriate" (March and Olsen 1996) in governing. Thus, it is argued here that NPM fulfills exactly this function.

A further part of the "common knowledge" argument is that one of the reasons for the NPM's persistence is precisely connected to its so-called "linguistic and discursive hegemony." As Magalhães and Veiga observe (2018, 3), in public administration, "hegemonic discourses fix the meaning of concepts and notions and contribute to their normalization or naturalization." However, as the authors point out, "there is no definite hegemony of discourses [. . .] because it is always contingent"; moreover, different "discourses compete for hegemony and struggle to fix the meaning of good, effective, and efficient public administration." Davies and Chorianopoulos (2018, 5) challenge the assertion by Sørensen and Torfing (2018) that governance is now a mature paradigm with distinctive methods and theories – including those they helped to develop, such as metagovernance, collaboration, and cocreation. Davies and Chorianopoulos caution: "history tells us that paradigms have a life cycle. Eventually, they fade or are driven from the

---

the elements in the basket as, remaining in the metaphor, the NPM basket has been around for longer than the NPG one.

[10] The term "Latin of our times" is taken from Engwall (1992), who compares the language of business administration to Latin in the Middle Ages.

historical stage. Some are more durable than others, for a host of good and bad reasons [...] paradigms often outlive the historical conditions that gave rise to them, and survive only as 'zombie categories'." However, the point here is that NPM is not a "zombie category" at all, but a quite lively and operational category, even in terms of language and discourse.

The fourth reason refers to the "shortcomings' compensation/reduction" argument. The claim is that, in the governance hybrid largely formed by "layering or sedimentation" (Mahoney and Thelen 2010; Streeck and Thelen 2005), NPM is able to compensate for or at least reduce some of NPG's shortcomings.[11]

A first weakness of NPG compared to NPM is that the former, by creating complex plural arenas, is expensive because of higher "costs of management and staff time [...] sustaining cross-cutting working arrangements" (Pollitt 2003, 38). Instead, NPM would seem to offer a more streamlined, cost- and time-saving model. Actually, NPM also suffers from rather high transaction and coordination costs due to outsourcing and agencification strategies. In this perspective, the metagovernance *avant la lettre* of NPM (Torfing et al. 2012) is expensive and difficult too, but less than the NPG's one, which is aimed at networks not only complex but "plural."

A second weakness is that NPG "tends not to clarify the lines of accountability" (Christensen and Lægreid 2007a, 1063; Pollitt 2003). On the basis of Goodin's reasoning (2003), it can be contended that in NPG the point of reference in terms of accountability is unclear. While, accountability referents (accountees) are obvious in TPA and NPM (citizens-voters and politicians, outside the bureaucracies; and hierarchical supervisors/managers, inside), they are not equally manifest in NPG, especially as network governance. Indeed, as Klijn and Koppejan (2014, 8) observe, "the emergence of networks threatens the classical democratic institutions and their forms of accountability. This arises because if various societal actors are involved in the formulation (and implementation) of policy goals, as is the case in governance networks, the primacy of politics is challenged in one way or another." Furthermore, the reference to stakeholders complicates the matter, as their excessive number makes it impossible to identify them. The risk is, therefore, that being accountable to everyone means being accountable to no one.

Even the subject of accountability is hardly determinable and communicable. If, in TPA and NPM, the objects of accountability are, respectively, actions/procedures and results as outputs/products, in NPG, they should be "intentions"

---

[11] In the analysis developed here, some observations made by Christensen and Lægreid (2007a) and Pollitt (2003) on whole-of-government will be applied to NPG, constructing a new argument.

(Goodin 2003), that is, motivations for cooperation, and long-term outcomes. Thus, while leaving aside the difficult issue of "intentions," evaluating long-term outcomes remains a key concern regarding accountability in NPG. However, as Pollitt (2003, 8) points out about whole-of-government, NPG also faces a serious flaw: "a greater difficulty in measuring effectiveness and impact, because of the need to develop and maintain more sophisticated performance measurement systems."

Ultimately, also those who argue that NPG, collaborative governance, and networks can be accountable thanks to "adequate arrangements to combine both horizontal and vertical accountability mechanisms" (Klijn and Koppejan 2014, 2) and social accountability (inter al., Fox 2015; Hickey and King 2016; Schatz 2013; on accountability and collaborative governance, see also Bianchi et al. 2021; Sørensen and Torfing 2021b) have to admit that "from an accountability perspective, networks can be considered problematic," since "it is difficult to hold actors accountable for outcomes that are realized by various actors collaborating in processes that are opaque and hard to assess" (Klijn and Koppejan 2014, 2). Furthermore, "although collaborative governance holds a promise of enhancing public sector accountability, we should not forget that collaborative governance raises just as many accountability problems as it solves" (Sørensen and Torfing 2021a, 3).

Yet, not only accountability but also responsibility[12] problems are traceable in NPG.[13] As Zouridis and Leijtens (2021, 126) argue, "the [N]PG paradigm goes along with blurred and diffused responsibilities of actors that, in turn, cause responsibility gaps. These responsibility gaps may cause governance failure and, in turn, trigger blame games and accountability gaps that foster public dissatisfaction." Shortcomings like these, together with a lack of connection between law and public management theory, lead the authors to even worry about "a foreseeable crisis of the current [N]PG paradigm" (Zouridis and Leijtens 2021, 127).

---

[12] Accountability and responsibility are often used interchangeably, even if they are distinct concepts. Some scholars argue that responsibility includes accountability, while others affirm the opposite (inter al. Koppell 2005). Generally, a person is "responsible for something," while is "accountable to someone." Thus, the main difference between the two concepts is that "responsibility connotes personal causal influence on an event [. . .], but it does not subsume the existence of audience to observe individual that is crucial factor of accountability concept" (Han and Demircioglu 2016, 3). Finally, a reason for the proliferation of accountability literature is that accountability is an "ever-expanding" (Mulgan 2000) and "evocative concept that is all too easily used in political discourse and policy documents because it conveys an image of transparency and trustworthiness" (Bovens, Schillemans, and Hart, 2008, note 33, 226).

[13] For accountability problems, tensions, and paradoxes that can arise in collaborative contexts, see Lee and Ospina (2022).

In the end, "silo mentalities" exist for good reasons (Christensen and Lægreid 2007a): they guarantee the vertical and horizontal definition of the organizational boundaries and, with them, two key principles for modern organizations, division of labor and specialization. Furthermore, "traditional approaches to structuring by organizational 'silo' organization" have a clear benefit: "membership and loyalty to a single organization" (Pollitt 2003, 39).

Finally, a reason for NPM's persistence and dominance lies in the representation and role it assigns to the state, understood as the ensemble of public administrations, within the public sector: even in the governance hybrid illustrated here, NPM recognizes the state as having the identity of a complex and divisional but single organization that has the task of governing, that is, the role of "government" and metagovernor. The point is crucial and will be further developed in the conclusions, concentrating on its relevance to NPG.

8 Conclusions

The concluding remarks are divided into five subsections. They offer a recap of the main arguments; highlight the origins and complexities of administrative narratives' hybridity with special reference to NPG; reflect on possible reform scenarios; delve into the risks and dark sides of NPG and discuss its conditions for effectiveness as a democratic model of governance; and finally outline directions for future research.

8.1 Summary of the "NPG as a Hybrid" Arguments

The topic of the NPG-NPM relationship is a rather densely populated field of studies. In a cumulative conception of scientific research (Bouckaert 2017), this Element provides an original contribution to a central debate in public governance and public administration.

NPG has a reactive *origin* to NPM, but its oppositive nature has been overemphasized because NPG incorporates key elements of NPM, which not only persist but are still dominant.

The arguments in favor of the "continuity and hybridization" hypothesis and, more generally, of NPG as a hybrid are: first, NPG's criticism is mainly directed at one of the two main streams of NPM (managerialism), while the other stream (public choice) is the source of important elements of continuity and hybridization between NPG and NPM, such as interorganizational approach, but also polycentricity and coproduction. These theories are NPG's milestones, though the latter two have not been part of NPM; second, the "discursive object" from which NPG descends, the theory of governance, is an hybrid, since opposite concepts are traceable in it (e.g., market, NPM, and government); third, market does not disappear, but rather remains as an unavoidable piece of the (liberal) democratic, plural and pluralist construction of NPG; fourth, another key trait of NPM, consumerism, even expanded in NPG. Finally, the label "post-NPM" itself, associated with NPG as an umbrella term, contradicts the hypothesis of linear and radical transition.

The reasons for the hybridization of NPG with NPM are also fourfold: first, the so-called "structural compatibility" between NPM and NPG, since, simplifying, they have two different focuses ("inside" vs. "outside" of the bureaucratic organization); second, NPM and NPG have a history and key points in common, such as TPA, theory of governance, and – part of – public choice (the "continuity" argument); third, both NPM and NPG draw inspiration from the private world, namely, market organizations and civil society, respectively (the "inspiration from the 'private'" argument); fourth, the pragmatic union between NPG and NPM finds no effective opponents in political-administrative élites, mainly thanks to the "neutral" praxeological strength of NPM (the "lack of an effective opposition" argument). In addition to these four reasons, the "avoidance of blame" mechanism also contributes to the hybridization process.

Finally, the motivations for NPM's persistence and dominance are: first, hybridization with NPM is necessary to penetrate the operating core of public administration ("toolkit and TPA anchoring" argument); second, NPM has strong legs to walk, that is, managers ("legs" argument); third, NPM represents a common knowledge and vocabulary, shared by civil servants and scholars ("common knowledge" argument); fourth, NPM is able to compensate for/ reduce some of NPG's shortcomings: accountability, responsibility, transaction costs, and membership/identity problems ("shortcomings' compensation/ reduction" argument).

Thus, the value of this Element lies in an original construction of arguments aimed at taking a position in a debate of interest to a wide audience and in the development of a theoretical account for NPG that challenges part of previous understandings and research on the subject, disconfirming the idea of a radical subversion in the shift from NPM to NPG.

8.2 Administrative Narratives and Hybridity

In addition to the core value illustrated in the previous subsection of the conclusions, an original contribution of this Element is that, through the analysis of the NPG narrative as a management, governance, and reform tool, it provides some interpretive keys for understanding where the hybridity of administrative narratives comes from and how it takes shape.

Regarding the hybridity of administrative narratives and, in particular, of NPG, the key elements are two: narratives as collective coconstructions and the agency of the narrating actors.

This contribution shows how the initiator of NPG, Osborne (2006, 2010), acted as a narrative entrepreneur: he combined preexisting elements, and older and newer ideas, giving life to a new story.

Other hybridity is added to this initial hybridity as NPG, like all administrative narratives, is a collective coconstruction: other narrators have joined and continue to join the initial narrator, adding, modifying, removing, cutting out pieces of the first story, crafting versions that differ to a lesser or greater extent from the original one.

In this bricolage and "anarchic" process (of organizing) of the storytelling, the spatial and temporal context is fundamental: in different times and different countries, with different administrative traditions and political situations, different actors coconstruct different narrative versions.

However, "globalization drivers" are also important in narratives: actors use ideas and pieces of stories manufactured elsewhere, also thanks to the communication technology development. Therefore, in administrative narratives, allomorphic dynamics within isomorphic processes, that is, divergence in convergence, can be observed.

This intricate landscape of narrative construction gains further nuances when the role of mythologized ideas in creating global administrative trends is considered. In the arguments in favor of the convergence, that is of NPG as a "new global administrative trend," the mythical perspective is, of course, central (Christensen and Lægreid 2007a; Meyer and Rowan 1977). In this perspective, following what Christensen and Fan (2016, 6) say about the post-NPM, not only NPG would be "a strong counter-myth phenomenon," but its success, especially in terms of legitimacy, would be strictly linked to the previous myth, that one of the NPM, and its "demonization" (Goldfinch and Wallis 2010, 1112).

Nonetheless, a key point in this representation of the narrative hybridity is that the (situated and collective) agency of conarrating actors (including public administration scholars) is clearly at the center: they not only navigate but build and shape hybridity.

The account of hybridity presented here and throughout the Element reveals that the theoretical lens used draws from three other approaches besides the constructionist lesson: the (neo)institutionalist theories and the Multiple Streams Framework, but also The Advocacy Coalition Framework. As van Gestel et al. argue (2018), these approaches emphasize, in a different but complementary way, the crucial role of ideas, institutions, and timing, as well as of individual and collective agency.

If the influence of the former two approaches is quite evident in this Element, the role of The Advocacy Coalition Framework needs to be clarified. According to van Gestel and colleagues (2018, 89), "The ACF framework perceives 'ideas,' together with the coalitions of actors supporting them, as the driving forces." Actually, "ideas" and "actor coalitions" are key elements not only for explaining public sector reforms but also for understanding the success or failure of administrative narratives as management, governance, and reform tools, as well as their dynamics of hybridization.

In summary, this Element offers a nuanced understanding of the intricate interplay of ideas, actors, and contexts that shape the hybrid narratives in public administration, ultimately shedding light on the complexities and dynamism inherent in governance frameworks.

8.3 Reform Scenarios

Discussing the implementation of NPG as a management, governance, and reform narrative is beyond the scope of this contribution. However, some considerations on possible reform scenarios will be proposed here.

First of all, "convergence on ideas [and narratives] does not mean a convergence on design or practice" since "the power of ideas to drive reform can be limited by the interplay of politics, interests and institutions" (Goldfinch and Wallis 2010, 1104). Change is always context-related (Mahoney and Thelen 2010), and "the institutional dynamics of reforms can best be interpreted as a complex mixture of environmental pressure, polity features and historical institutional context" (Christensen and Lægreid 2007b, 4; see also Christensen and Lægreid 2011a, 138).

A second key point is that hybrid narratives are highly likely to produce hybrid "reform patterns" (Mahoney and Thelen 2010).

This second point leads us to the possible scenarios. Basically, three scenarios are outlined in the literature. The first one consists of the persistent and unchallenged dominance of NPM (Christensen and Lægreid 2007b, 24; Levy 2010[14]). The second one involves a restoration of the previous paradigm through a kind of pendulum swing back toward TPA (Christensen and Lægreid 2011, 130): "[NPM] rejection goes along with [TPA] resurrection" (Levy 2010, 237). Finally, the third one corresponds to a process of hybridization and "co-evolution of reform ideas" (Christensen and Lægreid 2007b, 24-24), the result being "a hybrid structure and culture" (Christensen and Lægreid 2011a, 130).

---

[14] Levy (2010, 236) distinguishes between NPM persistent dominance (i.e., status quo) and "intensification."

This Element clearly gives preference to the third scenario, that is, the hybridization of TPA, NPM, and NPG/post-NPM. Reasons against the other two scenarios are as follows: first, the NPM is not dead, but it has been widely challenged due to its failures; second, myths (such as NPM and TPA), but also countermyths (such as NPG), are resistant constructions and are likely to remain; third, the dismantling of older systems is difficult because it is expensive (Streeck and Thelen 2005, 22).

But, in hybrids, as Rhodes (2000, 346) says, "it's the mix that matters." So, which and how much TPA, NPM, and NPG will there be? Which elements will be institutionalized, and which will be de-institutionalized? Also, what will happen in NPM trailblazer and laggard countries? Which of the two effects will prevail: the swing-of-the-pendulum, so the adoption of NPG/post-NPM will be more significant where NPM has been adopted longer and more incisively, or the "cultural and institutional compatibility," so countries more reluctant to NPM will more easily implement NPG/post-NPM reforms? (see inter al. Hajnal and Rosta 2015)

It is not possible to give a definitive answer to these questions. Indeed, academics and "social sciences offer only provisional knowledge. Prediction is probably an impossibility, only hindsight is a realistic goal" (Rhodes 2000, 358).

In an imaginary poker game between NPG and NPM, NPG seems to have one less card in hand, that one of the toolbox, but compared to its rival, it also has a good card, that one of the values. Thus, NPG has an advantage in terms of governance legitimacy but is disadvantaged in terms of governance capacity.[15] However, NPG could play another card well: that one of "the governance of governance" (Torfing et al. 2012, 4). Indeed, a good metagovernance could allow an eclectic but orchestrated experimentation of different tools and solutions, including those of NPM, within a framework of shared values. Here, the challenge is to govern both the complexity and the hybridity[16] of today's organizations and society. Moreover, metagovernance as a governance of complexity and hybridity in a framework of shared (democratic) values strongly recalls the issue of the role of the state/government, as well as the crucial importance of its representations.

---

[15] About the two concepts, see inter al. Liu and Christensen (2022, 284).

[16] Christensen and Lægreid (2011b, 410) argue that complexity and hybridity are interrelated but distinct concepts: "The former has a structural dimension addressing vertical and horizontal specialization and a cultural dimension addressing the variety of informal norms and values. The latter addressing the potential tension or inconsistency between diverse structural and cultural elements."

Ultimately, while the complexities and variables at play make it impossible to predict future reforms, the necessity for a metagoverned approach remains clear. This underscores the pivotal role of the state in the complex and hybrid world of governance.

8.4 NPG as a Democratic Model of Governance: Risks and Conditions of Effectiveness

Moving to the end of conclusions, this subsection considers the risks and conditions of effectiveness of NPG as a democratic model of governance, especially as it promises a re-politicization and re-democratization of the public sector after what is widely recognized as a period of destructive dominance by NPM.

Actually, NPG and NPM are both governance and democratic narratives, at least in those countries that can be defined as liberal democracies. However, the NPG's democratic flavor is more than evident in considering its value and symbolic parts, such as participation and deliberation, as well as the promotion of a new public service ethos and cocreation of public value.

By accepting Selznick's (1949, 265) argument that the alternative to a critique which may often seem "conservative or pessimistic [...] is the transformation of democracy into a utopian notion which, unaware of its internal dangers, is unarmed to meet them," this contribution not only questions assumptions taken for granted (e.g., NPG's oppositive nature), highlighting latent dynamics (hybridization), but intends to address the possible dark side of NPG (see Osborne and Strokosch 2022, 190). Indeed, NPG, like post-NPM, is generally "seen as a good thing" but presents "difficulties" (Christensen and Lægreid 2007a, 1063), such as ambitious agendas, unintentional risks, ambiguities, and uncontrolled consequences (see also Perri 6 et al. 2002). Therefore, "we must critically evaluate whether NPG contributes to the production of effective, democratic, and innovative solutions to wicked problems" (Torfing and Triantafillou 2013, 22).

The main challenge faced by NPG is to keep its promise of search and (co-)production/creation of public value (Stoker 2006), at the same time preserving the public interest (Wise 2010). The key to meeting this challenge lies in the state's capacity to articulate and enforce a clear vision of governance, even *vis-à-vis* the difficult balance between negotiation and compromise inherent to multiple-stakeholder contexts. Failure on this front would mean leaving NPG "trapped in a normative bubble" (Davies and Chorianopoulos 2018, 5), where "the claims of added public value may be overstated" (Koppenjan and Koliba 2013, 2).

The great risk of NPG – as a governance hybrid largely shaped through layering and sedimentation (Mahoney and Thelen 2010; Streeck and Thelen 2005), as well as mere juxtaposition – is that NPG and NPM will not just cohabit, but rather – by relying on market and multi-stakeholder networks negotiations – connive in the public sector's deresponsibilization, in times of "permanent austerity" (Pierson 2001).[17] The deresponsibilization can lurk in a progressive shift of responsibility from regular producers to coproducers (Brudney and England 1983), which can turn into an improper delegation to citizens by institutions (Cataldi 2015; Cataldi and Cappellato 2020; Cataldi et al. 2021).

However, to avoid the risk of playing the role of those "morticians [. . .] too eager to bury men's hopes" mentioned by Gouldner (1955, 507), next to the perils and challenges of NPG, there are also some conditions for its effectiveness that deserve to be emphasized, as possible starting points for a *construens* part.

Regarding the conditions for NPG's effectiveness, the first key element is undoubtedly the need for administrative reform.

Although the prospect of an overall reform and a radical change may seem too difficult (see inter al. Capano 2003; Ingrams et al. 2020; Kickert 2011),[18] if not sometimes unrealistic (Capano 1992), the relationship between politicians and bureaucrats should remain a priority. More than a few scholars would consider the "bureaucratic politics" model (Mayntz and Scharpf 1975) more functional for NPG implementation rather than the "dualistic" perspective. Indeed, cohesive political-administrative élites, able to take responsibility for a shared line of action, could give NPG strong legs to walk.

Furthermore, a crucial area needing reform is the center-periphery relationship. While the tendency toward re-centralization is supported by post-NPM doctrines, it can also affect NPG and collaborative governance, especially in the face of "turbulent problems" such as the COVID-19 pandemic. However, such a trend should not reduce the effective room for action available to local authorities. Indeed, they are fundamental actors in what is arguably the arena of collaborative governance *par excellence*: local and territorial processes (see Ansell et al. 2021).

The second condition, instead, emerges from Pollitt's (2003, 39) suggestion "not to throw the baby [i.e., the virtues of TPA and NPM] out with the bath

---

[17] Davies and Chorianopoulos (2018, 4) observe: "austerity is an important factor in undermining the foundations of pluricentric network governance and of centralizing power in a variety of disciplinary neoliberal state apparatuses." Clearly, the war in Ukraine and the Israel-Hamas conflict have rendered the prospect of "permanent austerity" more tangible than ever, amplifying the urgency of these concerns.

[18] Hammerschmid et al. (2019, 401) comment: "administrative reforms are invariably multifaceted, combine rhetoric and practice, suffer from incomplete specification, and experience shifts in purpose during the implementation process."

water." Thus, even in collaboration, a good option would imply not only holding but also strengthening the "well-defined organizational boundaries" and clearer lines of accountability of NPM, as well as the idea of entrepreneurial administration (Osborne and Gaebler 1992). The latter has the advantage of reaffirming the government's responsibility and, at the same time, makes it possible to look to external processes beyond internal administration.

Lastly, as it is difficult for integrative leaders to naturally emerge from governance processes, the presence of pragmatic and capable policy entrepreneurs (Kingdon 1984) may represent a good starting point to increase the chances of success for NPG.

In conclusion, this subsection suggests that there are reasons to believe that hybridization with NPM is a condition for the effectiveness of NPG, even as a democratic model of governance.

8.5 Directions for Future Research

This Element ends with a final consideration regarding the need to re-politicize public administration as a field of study (see, inter al., Roberts 2018) and suggests directions for future research.

Looking at NPG as a narrative tool, oriented toward the management, governance, and reform of the public sector, which brings into play the issue of the state, is certainly a first step to re-politicize public administration. Especially if, as Peters et al. (2022, 4) state, in "the contemporary turn from government to governance," also NPG "unwillingly contributes to the de-politicization of public administration by arguing that the rise of networked forms of governance is a smart and efficient way of ensuring coordination and governability of our increasingly complex, fragmented and multilayered societies," in fact leaving politics and public bureaucracies aside. Of course, much remains to be done on this front, but metagovernance research looks promising.

Other directions for future research also seem fruitful. First, extend the study of hybridization trajectories to NWS. Second, investigate the different mixes of governance elements in different policy areas, also in a comparative perspective. Third, explore NPG in welfare governance, not only because the latter abounds in wicked issues, but to test the ability of NPG to challenge the so-called "neoliberal paradigm of control-surveillance" based on conditionality, citizen activation and responsibilization, and so on. Fourth, further investigate actors' agency to understand how they shape hybridity in practice (see Nielsen and Andersen 2022). Last but not least, promote a reflection on scholars' agency in constructing a plural and pluralist society.

References

Agranoff, Robert. 2006. Inside Collaborative Networks: Ten Lessons for Public Managers. *Public Administration Review* 66(S1): 56–65.

Agranoff, Robert, and Michael McGuire. 2003. *Collaborative Public Management: New Strategies for Local Governments*. Washington, DC: Georgetown University Press.

Almond, Gabriel A. 1988. The Return to the State. *The American Political Science Review* 82(3): 853–874.

Andresani, Gianluca, and Ewan Ferlie. 2006. Studying Governance within the British Public Sector and without. *Public Management Review* 8(3): 415–431.

Ansell, Chris, and Alison Gash. 2008. Collaborative Governance in Theory and Practice. *Journal of Public Administration Research and Theory* 18(4): 543–571.

Ansell, Christopher, Eva Sørensen, and Jacob Torfing. 2021. The COVID-19 Pandemic as a Game Changer for Public Administration and Leadership? The Need for Robust Governance Responses to Turbulent Problems. *Public Management Review* 23(7): 949–960.

Ansell, Christopher, and Jacob Torfing. 2021. A New Public Governance Based on Co-creation. In *Public Governance as Co-creation: A Strategy for Revitalizing the Public Sector and Rejuvenating Democracy*, 1–32. Cambridge: Cambridge University Press.

Aristovnik, Aleksander, Eva Murko, and Dejan Ravšelj. 2022. From Neo-Weberian to Hybrid Governance Models in Public Administration: Differences between State and Local Self-Government. *Administrative Sciences* 12(1): 26.

Aucoin, Peter. 1990. Administrative Reform in Public Management: Paradigms, Principles, Paradoxes and Pendulums. *Governance* 3(2): 115–137.

Barnard, Chester I. 1938. *The Functions of the Executive*. Cambridge, MA: Harvard University Press.

Bakvis, Herman, and Luc Juillet. 2004. *The Horizontal Challenge: Line Departments, Central Agencies and Leadership*. Ottawa: Canada School of Public Services.

Bass, Bernard M. 1985. *Leadership and Performance beyond Expectations*. New York: The Free Press.

Battilana, Julie, Marya Besharov, and Bjoern Mitzinneck. 2017. On Hybrids and Hybrid Organizing: A Review and Roadmap for Future Research. In *The Sage Handbook of Organizational Institutionalism* 2nd ed., eds., Royston Greenwood, Christine Oliver, Thomas B. Lawrence, and Renate E. Meyer, 128–162. Thousand Oaks, CA: SAGE.

Benington, John. 2011. From Private Choice to Public Value. In *Public Value Theory and Practice*, eds., John Benington and Mark Moore, 31–49. Basingstoke: Palgrave-MacMillan.

Benington, John, and Jean Hartley. 2009. *Whole Systems Go! Improving Leadership across the Whole Public Service System: Propositions to Stimulate Discussion and Reform*. Sunningdale: National School of Government Report.

Benn, Stanley I., and Gerald F. Gaus. 1983. *Public and Private in Social Life*. New York: St. Martin's Press.

Bevir, Mark, and Roderick A. W. Rhodes. 2003. *Interpreting British Governance*. London: Routledge.

Bevir, Mark, and Roderick A. W. Rhodes. 2006. *Governance Stories*. London: Routledge.

Bevir, Mark, and Roderick A. W. Rhodes. 2022. All You Need Is . . . a Network: The Rise of Interpretive Public Administration. *Public Administration* 100(1): 149–160.

Bianchi, Carmine, Greta Nasi, and William Rivenbark. 2021. Implementing Collaborative Governance: Models, Experiences, and Challenges. *Public Management Review* 23(11): 1581–1589.

Bogdanor, Vernon. 2005. *Joined-Up Government*. Oxford: Oxford University Press.

Bojang, Malang B. S. 2020. Beyond New Public Management Paradigm: The Public Value Paradigm and Its Implications for Public Sector Managers. *Global Journal of Management and Business Research* 20(12): 1–7.

Bono, Joice E., Winny Shen, and Mark Snyder. 2010. Fostering Integrative Community Leadership. *Journal of Public Administration Research and Theory* 21(2): 324–335.

Bouckaert, Geert. 2017. Taking Stock of "Governance": A Predominantly European Perspective. *Governance* 30: 45–52.

Bouckaert, Geert. 2022. The Neo-Weberian State: From Ideal Type Model to Reality?. Working Paper Series (IIPP WP 2022–10), UCL Institute for Innovation and Public Purpose, www.ucl.ac.uk/bartlett/public-purpose/wp2022-10.

Bovaird, Tony. 2007. Beyond Engagement and Participation: User and Community Coproduction of Public Services. *Public Administration Review* 67(5): 846–860.

Bovaird, Tony, and Elke Löffler. 2003. Evaluating the Quality of Public Governance: Indicators, Models and Methodologies. *International Review of Administrative Sciences* 69(3): 313–328.

Bovens, Mark, Thomas Schillemans, and Paul 'T Hart. 2008. Does Public Accountability Work? An Assessment Tool. *Public Administration* 86(1): 225–242.

Box, Richard C., Gary S. Marshall, B. J. Reed, and Christine M. Reed. 2001. New Public Management and Substantive Democracy. *Public Administration Review* 61(5): 608–619.

Boyne George A., Catherine Farrell, Jennifer Law, Martin Powell, and Richard Walker. 2003. *Evaluating Public Management Reforms*. Buckingham: Open University Press.

Bozeman, Barry. 1993. Theory, 'Wisdom', and the Character of Knowledge in Public Management. In *Public Management*, ed., Barry Bozeman, 27–39. San Francisco, CA: Jossey-Bass.

Brandsen, Taco. 2010. Hybridity/Hybridization. In *International Encyclopedia of Civil Society*, eds., Helmut K. Anheier, and Stefan Toepler, 839–842. New York: Springer.

Brandsen, Taco, Wim van de Donk, and Kim Putters. 2005. Griffins or Chameleons? Hybridity as a Permanent and Inevitable Characteristic of the Third Sector. *International Journal of Public Administration* 28: 749–765.

Brudney, Jeffrey L., and Robert E. England. 1983. Toward a Definition of the Coproduction Concept. *Public Administration Review* 43(1): 59–65.

Bryson, John M., Barbara C. Crosby, and Melissa Middleton Stone. 2006. The Design and Implementation of Cross-Sector Collaboration: Propositions from the Literature. *Public Administration Review* 66(S1): 44–55.

Burns, James McGregor. 1978. *Leadership*. New York: Harper & Row.

Caiden, Gerald E. 1969. *Administrative Reform*. Chicago, IL: Aldine.

Cairney, Paul, and Nikolaos Zahariadis. 2016. Multiple Streams Approach: A Flexible Metaphor Presents an Opportunity to Operationalize Agenda Setting Processes. In *Handbook of Public Policy Agenda Setting*, ed., Nikolaos Zahariadis, 87–105. Cheltenham: Edward Elgar.

Capano, Giliberto. 1992. *Improbabile riforma. Le politiche di riforma amministrativa nell'Italia repubblicana*. Bologna: Il Mulino.

Capano, Giliberto. 2003. Administrative Traditions and Policy Change: When Policy Paradigms Matter. The Case of Italian Administrative Reform during the 1990s. *Public Administration* 81: 781–801.

Capano, Giliberto, Michael Howlett, and M. Ramesh. 2015. Re-Thinking Governance in Public Policy: Dynamics, Strategy and Capacities. In *Varieties of Governance*, eds., Giliberto Capano, Michael Howlett, and M. Ramesh, 1–24. London: Palgrave Macmillan.

Cataldi, Laura. 2015. Coproduzione: Uno strumento di riforma in tempi di austerity? *Rivista Italiana di Politiche Pubbliche* 1: 59–86.

Cataldi, Laura. 2017. I "nuovi" servizi sociali: vecchio managerialismo e moderna burocratizzazione. In *Logica professionale e logica manageriale. Una ricerca sulle professioni sociali*, eds., Willem Tousijn, and Marilena Dellavalle, 41–94. Il Mulino: Bologna.

Cataldi, Laura, and Francesca Tomatis. 2022. Gender and Professionalism: Still a Black Box. A Call for Research, Debate and Action. Suggestions from and beyond the Pandemic Crisis. *Organization* 0(0). https://doi.org/10.1177/13505084221115835.

Cataldi, Laura, and Valeria Cappellato. 2020. New Welfare Narratives in Italy: Risks and Supposed Virtues. *The Tocqueville Review/ La Revue Tocqueville* 41(1): 207–250.

Cataldi, Laura, and Willem Tousijn. 2015. Quale managerialismo nei servizi sociali? Considerazioni critiche. *Polis* 2: 157–190.

Cataldi, Laura, Francesca Tomatis, and Giuliana Costa. 2021. Even More in the Pandemic and Social Emergency: For an Individual Welfare beyond the Family and the Community. *Community, Work & Family*. https://doi.org/10.1080/13668803.2021.1911936.

Christensen, Tom. 2012. Post-NPM and Changing Public Governance. *Meiji Journal of Political Science and Economics* 1: 1–11.

Christensen, Tom, and Per Lægreid. 2006. The Whole-of-Government Approach – Regulation, Performance, and Public-Sector Reform. Working Paper 6, Stein Rokkan Centre For Social Studies, August.

Christensen, Tom, and Per Lægreid. 2007a. The Whole-of-Government Approach to Public Sector Reform. *Public Administration Review* 67(6): 1059–1066.

Christensen, Tom, and Per Lægreid. 2007b. *Trascending New Public Management: The Transformation of Public Sector Reforms*. London: Routledge.

Christensen, Tom, and Per Lægreid. 2011a. Democracy and Administrative Policy: Contrasting Elements of New Public Management (NPM) and Post-NPM. *European Political Science Review* (3)1: 125–146.

Christensen, Tom, and Per Lægreid. 2011b. Complexity and Hybrid Public Administration: Theoretical and Empirical Challenges. *Public Organization Review* 11(4): 407–423.

Christensen, Tom, and Yongmao Fan. 2016. Post-New Public Management: A New Administrative Paradigm for China? *International Review of Administrative Sciences* 84(2): 1–16.

Clark, David (1996). Open Government in Britain: Discourse and Practice. *Public Money & Management* 16(1): 23–30.

Clarke, John H. 1996. After Social Work. In *Social Theory, Social Change and Social Work*, ed., Nigel Parton, 36–60. London: Routledge.

Considine, Mark, and Jennifer M. L. Lewis. 2003. Bureaucracy, Network or Enterprise? Comparing Models of Governance in Australia, Britain, the Netherlands, and New Zealand. *Public Administration Review* 63(2): 131–140.

Crosby, Barbara C., and Bryson John M. 2005. A Leadership Framework for Cross-Sector Collaboration. *Public Management Review* 7(2): 177–201.

Crosby, Barbara C., and John M. Bryson. 2010. Integrative Leadership and the Creation and Maintenance of Cross-Sector Collaborations. *Journal of Public Administration Research and Theory* 21(2): 211–230.

Crouch, Colin. 2005. *Capitalist Diversity and Change: Recombinant Governance and Institutional Entrepreneurs*. Oxford: Oxford University Press.

Dalingwater, Louise. 2014. Post-new Public Management (NPM) and the Reconfiguration of Health Services in England. *Observatoire de la Société Britannique* 16: 51–64.

Davies, Jonathan S., and Ioannis Chorianopoulos. 2018. Governance: Mature Paradigm or Chicken Soup for European Public Management? *Critical Policy Studies* 12(3): 360–366.

de Vries, Hanna, Lars Tummers, and Victor Bekkers. 2018. The Diffusion and Adoption of Public Sector Innovations: A Meta-Synthesis of the Literature. *Perspectives on Public Management and Governance* 1(3): 159–176.

de Vries, Jouke. 2010. Is New Public Management Really Dead? *OECD Journal on Budgeting* 10(1): 1–5. https://doi.org/10.1787/budget-10-5km8xx3mp60n.

Denhardt, Robert B., and Janet V. Denhardt. 2000. The New Public Service: Serving Rather than Steering. *Public Administration Review* 60(6): 549–559.

Denis, Jean-Louis, Ann Langley, and Viviane Sergi. 2012. Leadership in the Plural. *The Academy of Management Annals* 6(1): 211–283.

Denis, Jean-Louis, Ewan Ferlie, and Nicolette Van Gestel. 2015. Understanding Hybridity in Public Organizations. *Public Administration* 93: 273–289.

Dickinson, Helen. 2016. From New Public Management to New Public Governance: The Implications for a "New Public Service". In *The Three Sector Solution: Delivering Public Policy in Collaboration with No-for-Profits and Business*, eds., John R. Butcher, and David J. Gilchrist, 41–60. Canberra: ANU Press.

DiMaggio, Paul J., and Walter W. Powell. 1983. The Iron Cage Revisited. *American Sociological Review* 48: 147–160.

Dunleavy, Patrick, and Christopher Hood. 1994. From Old Public Administration to New Public Management. *Public Money & Management* 14(3): 9–16.

Dunleavy, Patrick, Helen Margetts, Simon Bastow, and Jane Tinkler. 2006. New Public Management is Dead – Long Live Digital-Era Governance. *Journal of Public Administration Research and Theory* 16(3): 467–494.

Dunn, William. 1981. *Public Policy Analysis: An Introduction*. Englewood Cliffs, NJ: Prentice Hall.

Easton, David. 1953. *The Political System: An Inquiry into the State of Political Science*. New York: Alfred A. Knopf.

Edwards, J. David. 1998. Managerial Influences in Public Administration. *International Journal of Organization Theory & Behavior* 1(4): 553–583.

Emerson, Kirk, Tina Nabatchi, and Stephen Balogh. 2012. An Integrative Framework for Collaborative Governance. *Journal of Public Administration Research and Theory* 22(1): 1–29.

Engwall, Lars. 1992. *Mercury Meets Minerva: Business Studies and Higher Education: The Swedish Case*. London: Pergamon Press.

Entwistle, Tom, and Steve Martin. 2005. From Competition to Collaboration in Public Service Delivery: A New Agenda for Research. *Public Administration* 83(1): 233–242.

Eymeri-Douzans, Jean-Michel. 2013. Administrative Reforms: Is France within the World Movement? In *La France et ses administrations. Un état des savoirs/ France and Its Public Administrations: A State of the Art*, eds., Jean-Michel Eymeri-Douzans, and Geert Bouckaert, 497–519. Brussels: Bruylant.

Fattore, Giovanni, Hans F. W Dubois, and Antonio Lapenta. 2012. Measuring New Public Management and Governance in Political Debate. *Public Administration Review* 72(2): 218–227.

Ferlie Ewan, Christine Musselin, and Gianluca Andresani. 2009. The Governance of Higher Education Systems: A Public Management Perspective. In *University Governance: Western European Comparative Perspective*, eds., Catherine Paradeise, Emanuela Reale, Ivar Bleiklie, and Ewan Ferlie, 1–19. Dordrecht: Springer.

Fox, Jonathan A. 2015. Social Accountability: What Does the Evidence Really Say? *World Development* 72: 346–361.

Getha-Taylor, Heater. 2009. Managing the "New Normalcy" with Values-Based Leadership: Lessons from Admiral James Loy. *Public Administration Review* 69(2): 200–206.

Gherardi, Silvia, and Bengt Jacobsson. 2000. Managerialese as the Latin of Our Times: Reforming Italian Public Sector Organizations. *Scandinavian Journal of Management* 16: 349–355.

Giddens, Anthony. 1984. *The Constitution of Society: Outline of the Theory of Structuration*. Berkeley, CA: University of California Press.

Giddens, Anthony. 1998. *The Third Way: The Renewal of Social Democracy*. Cambridge, MA: Polity Press.

Girotti, Fiorenzo. 2007. *Amministrazioni pubbliche. Una introduzione*. Roma: Carocci.

Glynn, Mary Ann, Elisabeth A. Hood, and Benjamin D. Innis. 2020. Taking Hybridity for Granted: Institutionalization and Hybrid Identification. In *Organizational Hybridity: Perspectives, Processes, Promises* (Research in the Sociology of Organizations, Vol. 69), eds., Marya L. Besharov, and Bjoern C. Mitzinneck, 53–72. Bingley: Emerald.

Goldfinch, Shaun and Joe Wallis. 2010. Two Myths of Convergence in Public Management Reform. *Public Administration* 88: 1099–1115.

Goodin, Robert E. 2003. Democratic Accountability: The Distinctiveness of the Third Sector. *European Journal of Sociology* 44(3): 359–396.

Goodrick, Elizabeth, and Trish Reay. 2011. Constellations of Institutional Logics: Changes in the Professional Work of Pharmacists. *Work and Occupations* 38(3): 372–416.

Gouldner, Alvin W. 1955. Metaphysical Pathos and the Theory of Bureaucracy. *The American Political Science Review* 49(2): 496–507.

Gregory, Robert. 2003. All the King's Horses and All the King's Men: Putting New Zealand's Public Sector Back Together Again. *International Public Management Review* 4(2): 41–58.

Hajnal, György, and Miklos Rosta. 2015. NPM and Post-NPM in the View of European Administrative Elites: Towards Understanding the Relationship of Public Management Reform Doctrines. IRSPM Conference Paper, March 30–April 1, Birmingham.

Halligan, John (2006). The Reassertion of the Centre in a First Generation NPM System. In *Autonomy and Regulation: Coping with Agencies in the Modern State*, ed., Tom Christensen, and Per Lægreid, 162–180, Cheltenham: Edward Elgar.

Halligan, John. 2007. Reintegrating Government in Third-Generation Reforms of Australia and New Zealand. *Public Policy and Administration* 22(2): 217–238. https://doi.org/10.1177/0952076707075899.

Halligan, John. 2010. Post-NPM Responses to Disaggregation through Coordinating Horizontally and Integrating Governance. In *Governance of Public Sector Organizations: Governance and Public Management*, eds., Per Lægreid, and Koen Verhoest, 235–254. London: Palgrave Macmillan.

Hammerschmid, Gerhard, Steven Van de Walle, Rhys Andrews, and Ahmed M. S. Mostafa. 2019. New Public Management Reforms in Europe and Their Effects: Findings from a 20-Country Top Executive Survey. *International Review of Administrative Sciences* 85(3): 399–418.

Han, Yousueng, and Mehemet A. Demircioglu. 2016. Accountability, Politics, and Power. In *Global Encyclopedia of Public Administration, Public Policy, and Governance*, ed. Farazmand, A. Cham: Springer. https://doi.org/10.1007/978-3-319-31816-5_2453-2.

Hart, Paul T., and John Uhr. 2008. *Public Leadership: Perspectives and Practices*. Canberra: ANU Press.

Hay, Colin. 2004. Ideas, Interests and Institutions in the Comparative Political Economy of Great Transformations. *Review of International Political Economy* 11(1): 204–226.

Haynes, Philip. 2003. *Managing Complexity in the Public Services*. Maidenhead: Open University Press.

Head, Brian W., and John Alford. 2015. Wicked Problems: Implications for Public Policy and Management. *Administration & Society* 47(6): 711–739. https://doi.org/10.1177/0095399713481601

Hickey, Sam, and Sophie King. 2016. Understanding Social Accountability: Politics, Power and Building New Social Contracts. *The Journal of Development Studies* 52: 1225–1240

Hjern, Benny, and David O. Porter. 1981. Implementation Structures: A New Unit of Administrative Analysis. *Organization Studies* 2(3): 211–227.

Hood, Christopher. 1991. A Public Management for All Seasons? *Public Administration* 69: 3–19.

Hood, Christopher, and Guy Peters. 2004. The Middle Ageing of New Public Management: Into an Age of Paradox? *Journal of Public Administration Research and Theory* 14(3): 267–282.

Hood, Christopher, and Ruth Dixon. 2015a. A Government that Worked Better and Cost Less? Evaluating Three Decades of Reform and Change in UK Central Government. New York: Oxford University Press.

Hood, Christopher, and Ruth Dixon. 2015b. What We Have to Show for 30 Years of New Public Management: Higher Costs, More Complaints. *Governance* 28(3): 265–267.

Hyndman, Noel, and Irvine Lapsley. 2016. New Public Management: The Story Continues. *Financial Accountability & Management* 32(4): 385–408.

Hyndman, Noel, and Mariannunziata Liguori. 2016. Public Sector Reforms: Changing Contours on an NPM Landscape. *Financial Accountability and Management* 32(1): 5–32.

Ingrams, Alex, Suzanne Piotrowski, and Daniel Berliner. 2020. Learning from Our Mistakes: Public Management Reform and the Hope of Open Government. *Perspectives on Public Management and Governance* 3(4): 257–272.

Jann, Werner W. 2003. State, Administration and Governance in Germany: Competing Traditions and Dominant Narratives. *Public Administration* 81: 95–118.

Jessop, Robert. 2002. Governance, Governance Failure, Meta-governance. In *Participatory Governance in Multi-Level Context: Concepts and Experience*, ed., Hubert Heinelt, 33–58. Opladen: Leske and Budrich.

Jones, Candace, William S. Hesterly, and Stephen P. Borgatti. 1997. A General Theory of Network Governance: Exchange Conditions and Social Mechanisms. *The Academy of Management Review* 22(4): 911–945.

Karataş, Adnan. 2019. Post-New Public Management Paradigm and Its Effects on Public Administration. *Social Mentality and Researcher Thinkers Journal* 5(26): 1796–1805.

Keast, Robyn, Myrna Mandell, and Kerry Brown. 2006. Mixing State, Market, and Network Governance Modes: The Role of Government in "Crowded" Policy Domains. *International Journal of Organizational Theory and Behaviour* 9(1): 27–50.

Keast, Robyn, Kerry Brown, and Myrna Mandell. 2007. Getting the Right Mix: Unpacking Integration Meanings and Strategies. *International Public Management Journal* 10(1): 9–33. doi:10.1080/10967490601185716.

Kettl, Donald F. 1993. *Sharing Power: Public Governance and Private Markets*. Washington, DC: The Brookings Institution.

Kettl, Donald F. 2006. Managing Boundaries in American Administration. *Public Administration Review* 66: 10–19.

Kickert, Walter. 2011. Distinctiveness of Administrative Reform in Greece, Italy, Portugal and Spain. Common Characteristics of Context, Administrations and Reforms. *Public Administration* 89: 801–818.

Kickert, Walter J. M., Erik-Hans Klijn, and Joop F.M. Koppenjan. 1997. *Managing Complex Networks*. London: SAGE.

Kinder, Tony. 2012. Learning, Innovating and Performance in Post-new Public Management of Locally Delivered Public Services. *Public Management Review* 14(3): 403–428.

Kingdon, John W. 1984. *Agendas, Alternatives, and Public Policies*. Boston, MA: Little, Brown.

Klenk, Tanja, and Renate Reiter. 2019. Post-New Public Management: Reform Ideas and Their Application in the Field of Social Services. *International Review of Administrative Sciences* 85(1): 3–10.

Klijn, Erik-Hans, and Joop F. M. Koppenjan. 2000. Public Management and Policy Networks. *Public Management* 2(2): 135–158.

Klijn, Erik-Hans., and Joop F. M. Koppenjan. 2004. *Managing Uncertainties in Networks*. London: Routledge.

Klijn, Erik-Hans, and Joop F. M. Koppenjan. 2014. Accountable Networks. In *The Oxford Handbook of Public Accountability*, eds., Mark Bovens, Robert Goodin, and Thomas Schillemans, 242–257. Oxford: Oxford Academic.

Koliba, Christopher J., Jack W. Meek, and Asim Zia. 2010. *Governance Networks in Public Administration and Public Policy*. Boca Raton, FL: Taylor & Francis.

Kooiman, Jan. 1993. *Modern Governance: New Government-Society Interactions*. Rotterdam: Erasmus University.

Kooiman, Jan. 2003. *Governing as Governance*. London: Sage.

Koppell, Jonathan G. S. 2005. Pathologies of Accountability: ICANN and the Challenge of "Multiple Accountabilities Disorder." *Public Administration Review* 65(1): 94–108.

Koppenjan, Joop. 2012. *The New Public Governance in Public Service Delivery*. The Hague: Eleven.

Koppenjan, Joop, and Christopher J. Koliba. 2013. Transformations towards New Public Governance: Can the New Paradigm Handle Complexity? *International Review of Public Administration* 2(18): 1–8.

Krlev, Gorgi, and Helmut K. Anheier. 2020. Hybridity. Origins and Effects. In *The Routledge Companion to Nonprofit Management*, eds. Helmut K. Anheier and Stefan Toepler. Abingdon: Routledge, Routledge Handbooks Online. See: www.routledgehandbooks.com/doi/10.4324/9781315181011-40.

Krogh, Andreas Hagedorn, Annika Agger, and Peter Triantafillou. 2022. *Public Governance in Denmark: Meeting the Global Mega-Challenges of the 21st Century?* Bingley: Emerald Group.

Lapuente, Victor, and Steven Van de Walle. 2020. The Effects of New Public Management on the Quality of Public Services. *Governance* 33: 461–475.

Lee, Seulki, and Sonia M. Ospina. 2022. A Framework for Assessing Accountability in Collaborative Governance: A Process-Based Approach. *Perspectives on Public Management and Governance* 5(1): 63–75.

Levy, Roger. 2010. New Public Management: End of an Era? *Public Policy and Administration* 25(2): 234–240.

Liddle, Joyce. 2018. Public Value Management and New Public Governance: Key Traits, Issues and Developments. In *The Palgrave Handbook of Public Administration and Management in Europe*, eds., Edoardo Ongaro, and Sandra Van Thiel, 967–990. London: Palgrave Macmillan.

Lindquist, Evert. 2009. Waiting for the Next Wave: Trajectories, Narratives and Conveying the State of Public Sector Reform. *Policy Quarterly* 5(1): 44–52.

Liu, Yihong, and Tom Christensen. 2022. The Long-Term Development of Crisis Management in China: Continuity, Institutional Punctuations and Reforms. *Review of Policy Research* 39(3): 282–302.

Lynn, Laurence E. 2008. What is a Neo-Weberian State? Reflections on a Concept and Its Implications. *The NISPAcee Journal of Public Administration and Policy* 1(2): 17–30.

Magalhães, António, and Amélia Veiga. 2018. Narrative of Governance. In *Global Encyclopedia of Public Administration, Public Policy, and Governance*, ed., Ali Farazmand, 1–5. Cham: Springer. https://doi.org/ 10.1007/978-3-319-31816-5_3136-1.

Mahoney, James, and Kathleen Thelen. 2010. *Explaining Institutional Change: Ambiguity, Agency, and Power*. Cambridge: Cambridge University Press.

March, James, and Johan P. Olsen. 1996. Institutional Perspectives on Political Institutions. *Governance* 9(3): 247–64. https://doi.org/10.1111/j.1468-0491.1996.tb00242.x.

Margetts, Helen, and Patrick Dunleavy. 2013. The Second Wave of Digital-Era Governance: A Quasi-Paradigm for Government on the Web. *Philosophical Transactions of the Royal Society A* 371: 1–17. http://doi.org/10.1098/ rsta.2012.0382.

Massey, Andrew. 2019. Persistent Public Management Reform: An Egregore of Liberal Authoritarianism? *Public Money & Management* 39(1): 9–17.

Mathias H., Nielsen, and Niklas Andersen. 2022. From Coping to Co-Construction. A New Approach to Studying How Public Officials Shape Hybrid Forms of Governance. ESPAnet Conference Paper, Vienna, September 14–16.

Maynard-Moody, Steven, and Michael Musheno. 2000. State Agent or Citizen Agent: Two Narratives of Discretion. *Journal of Public Administration Research and Theory* 10(2): 329–358.

Mayntz, Renate, and Fritz W Scharpf. 1975. *Policy-Making in the German Federal Bureaucracy*. New York: Elsevier.

McGinnis, Michael D. 1999. Polycentricity and Local Public Economies: Readings from the Workshop in Political Theory and Policy Analysis. Ann Arbor, MI: University of Michigan Press.

McGuire, Michael. 2006. Collaborative Public Management: Assessing What We Know and How We Know It. *Public Administration Review* 66(s1): 33–43.

McNamara, Madeleine. 2012. Starting to Untangle the Web of Cooperation, Coordination, and Collaboration: A Framework for Public Managers. *International Journal of Public Administration* 35 (6): 389–401.

Meyer, John, and Brian Rowan. 1977. Institutionalized Organizations: Formal Structure as Myth and Ceremony. *American Journal of Sociology* 83(2): 340–363.

Mills, David Ernest, Lisa Bradley, and Robyn Keast. 2021. NPG and Stewardship Theory: Remedies for NPM Privatization Prescriptions. *Public Management Review* 23(4): 501–522.

Milward, H. Brinton, Laura Jensen, Alasdair Roberts et al. 2016. Is Public Management Neglecting the State? *Governance* 29(3): 1–26.

Mintrom, Michael, and Ruby O'Connor. 2020. The Importance of Policy Narrative: Effective Government Responses to Covid-19. *Policy Design and Practice* 3(3): 205–227.

Moore, Mark H. 1995. *Creating Public Value*. Cambridge, MA: Harvard University Press.

Morse, Ricardo. 2007. Developing Public Leaders in an Age of Collaborative Governance. Leading the Future of the Public Sector Conference Paper, University of Delaware, Newark, May 31–June 2.

Morse, Ricardo S. 2010. Integrative Public Leadership: Catalyzing Collaboration to Create Public Value. *The Leadership Quarterly* 21(2): 231–245.

Moulton, Stephanie. 2009. Putting together the Publicness Puzzle: A Framework for Realized Publicness. *Public Administration Review* 69(5): 889–900.

Mulgan, Geoff. 2005. Joined-Up Government: Past, Present, and Future. In *Joined-Up Government*, ed., Vernon Bogdanor, 175–187. Oxford: Oxford University Press.

Mulgan, Richard. 2000. "Accountability": An Ever-Expanding Concept? *Public Administration* 78(3): 555–573.

Needham, Catherine. 2015. Public Administration. In *The Handbook of Interpretive Political Science*, eds., Mark Bevir and Roderick Rhodes, 338–351. London: Routledge.

Newman, Janet E. 2001. *Modernising Governance: New Labour, Policy and Society*. London: SAGE.

O'Flynn, Janine. 2007. From New Public Management to Public Value: Paradigmatic Change and Managerial Implications. *Australian Journal of Public Administration* 66(3): 353–366.

O'Flynn, Janine. 2009. The Cult of Collaboration in Public Policy. *Australian Journal of Public Administration* 68(1): 112–116.

Ongaro, Edoardo. 2009. *Public Management Reform and Modernization: Trajectories of Administrative Change in Italy, France, Greece, Portugal and Spain.* Cheltenham: Edward Elgar.

Osborne, David, and Ted Gaebler. 1992. *Reinventing Government: How the Entrepreneurial Spirit is Transforming the Public Sector.* New York: Addison-Wesley.

Osborne, Stephen P. 2006. The New Public Governance. *Public Management Review* 8(3): 377–387.

Osborne, Stephen P. 2010. *New Public Governance? Emerging Perspectives on the Theory and Practice of Public Governance.* London: Routledge.

Osborne, Stephen P., and Kirsty Strokosch. 2022. Participation: Add-on or Core Component of Public Service Delivery? *Australian Journal of Public Administration* 81: 181–200.

Ospina, Sonia, and Enrica Foldy. 2010. Building Bridges from the Margins: The Work of Leadership in Social Change Organizations. *Journal of Public Administration Research and Theory* 21(2): 292–307.

Ostrom, Elinor. 1996. Crossing the Great Divide: Coproduction, Synergy and Development. *World Development* 24(6): 1073–1087.

Ostrom, Elinor. 2005. *Understanding Institutional Diversity.* Princeton, NJ: Princeton University Press.

Ostrom, Vincent. 1972. Polycentricity. Workshop Working Paper Series, Workshop in Political Theory and Policy Analysis, Presented at the Annual Meeting of the American Political Science Association, September 5–9.

Ostrom, Vincent, and Elinor Ostrom. 1965. A Behavioral Approach to the Study of Intergovernmental Relations. *Annals of the American Academy of Political and Social Science* 359(1): 135–146.

Ostrom, Vincent, and Elinor Ostrom. 1971. Public Choice: A Different Approach to the Study of Public Administration. *Public Administration Review* 31(2): 203–216.

Ostrom, Vincent, and Elinor Ostrom. 1977. Public goods and public choices. In *Alternatives for Delivering Public Services: Toward Improved Performance*, ed. Emanuel S. Savas, 7–49. Westview Special Studies in Public Systems Management. Boulder, Colorado: Westview Press.

Ostrom, Vincent, and Elinor Ostrom. 1999. Public Goods and Public Choices. *Polycentricity and Local Public Economies: Readings from the Workshop in*

Political Theory and Policy Analysis. Ann Arbor: The University of Michigan Press. 75–79.

Ostrom, Vincent, Charles M. Tiebout, and Robert Warren. 1961. The Organization of Government in Metropolitan Areas: A Theoretical Inquiry. *American Political Science Review* 55(4): 831–842.

Page, Stephen B. 2010. Integrative Leadership for Collaborative Governance: Civic Engagement in Seattle. *Journal of Public Administration Research and Theory* 21(2): 248–263.

Parks, Roger B., Paula C. Baker, Larry Kiser et al. 1981. Consumers as Coproducers of Public Services: Some Economic and Institutional Considerations. *Policy Studies Journal* 9(7): 1001–1011.

Perry, 6, Diana Leat, Kimberly Seltzer, and Gerry Stoker. 2002. *Towards Holistic Governance: The New Reform Agenda*. Houndmills: Palgrave Macmillan.

Peters, B. Guy. 2017. What Is So Wicked about Wicked Problems? A Conceptual Analysis and a Research Program. *Policy and Society* 36(3): 385–396.

Peters, B. Guy., Jon Pierre, Eva Sørensen, and Jacob Torfing. 2022. Bringing Political Science Back into Public Administration Research. *Governance* Online Version: 1–22.

Pestoff, Victor. 2006. Citizens and Co-production of Welfare Services. *Public Management Review* 8(4): 503–519.

Pestoff, Victor. 2012. New Public Governance, Co-production and Third Sector Social Services in Europe: Crowding in and Crowding Out. In *New Public Governance, the Third Sector and Co-Production*, eds., Victor Pestoff, Taco Brandsen, and Bram Verschuere, 13–34. London: Routledge.

Pierre, Jon, and B. Guy Peters. 2000. *Governance, Politics and the State*. New York: St. Martin's Press.

Pierson, Paul. 2001. Coping with Permanent Austerity: Welfare State Restructuring in Affluent Democracies. In *The New Politics of the Welfare State*, ed., Paul Pierson, 410–456. Oxford: Oxford University Press.

Pollitt, Christopher. 1990. *Managerialism and the Public Services: The Anglo-American Experience*. Oxford: Blackwell.

Pollitt, Christopher. 1995. Justification by Works or by Faith? Evaluating the New Public Management. *Evaluation* 1(2): 133–154.

Pollitt, Christopher. 2003. Joined-up Government: A Survey. *Political Studies Review* 1: 34–49.

Pollitt, Christopher, and Geert Bouckaert. 2004. *Public Management Reform. A Comparative Analysis*. 2nd ed., Oxford: Oxford University Press.

Pollitt, Christopher, and Geert Bouckaert. 2011. *Public Management Reform: A Comparative Analysis – New Public Management, Governance, and the Neo–Weberian State*. 3rd ed., Oxford: Oxford University Press.

Polzer, Tobias, Renate E. Meyer, Markus A. Höllerer, and Johann Seiwald. 2016. Institutional Hybridity in Public Sector Reform. In *How Institutions Matter!* eds., Joel Gehman, Michael Lounsbury, and Royston Greenwood, 69–99, Bingley: Emerald.

Powell, Martin, Ian Greener, Isabelle Szmigin, Shane Doheny, and Nick Mills. 2010. Broadening the Focus of Public Service Consumerism. *Public Management Review* 12(3): 323–339.

Powell, Walter W. 1990. Neither Market nor Hierarchy: Network Forms of Organization. *Research in Organizational Behavior* 12: 295–336.

Randma-Liiv, Tiina, and Wolfgang Drechsler. 2017. Three Decades, Four Phases: Public Administration Development in Central and Eastern Europe, 1989–2017. *International Journal of Public Sector Management* 30(6/7): 595–605.

Reinholde, Iveta, Arvydas Guogis, Vainius Smalskys, Skaidrė Žičkienė, and Daniel Klimovsky. 2020. Considering New Public Governance Possibilities in Central and Eastern Europe. *Tiltai* 2: 1–15.

Rhodes, Roderick A. W. 2000. The Governance Narrative: Key Findings and Lessons from the Erc's Whitehall Programme. *Public Administration* 78(2): 345–363.

Rhodes, Roderick A. W. 2019. Public Administration, the Interpretive Turn and Storytelling. In *A Research Agenda for Public Administration*, ed., Andrew Massey, 12–27. Cheltenham: Edward Elgar.

Roberts, Alasdair. 2018. The Aims of Public Administration: Reviving the Classical View. *Perspectives on Public Management and Governance* 1(1): 73–85.

Robinson, Mark. 2015. *From Old Public Administration to the New Public Service: Implications for Public Sector Reform in Developing Countries.* Singapore: UNDP Global Centre for Public Service Excellence.

Sabatier, Paul A., and Hank Jenkins-Smith. 1993. *Policy Change and Learning: An Advocacy Coalition Approach.* New York: Westview Press.

Salamon, Lester M. 2001. The New Governance and the Tools of Public Action: An Introduction. *Fordham Journal of Urban Law* XXVIII(5): 1611–1674.

Sardoni, Claudio. 2015. Opening the "Black Box" of the State. 19th FMM Conference, Berlin October 22–24.

Sartori, Giovanni. 1970. Concept Misinformation and Comparative Politics. *American Political Science Review* 64: 1033–1053.

Sartori, Giovanni. 1973. What Is "Politics." *Political Theory* 1(1): 5–26.

Scharpf, Fritz W. 1994. Games Real Actors Could Play: Positive and Negative Coordination in Embedded Negotiations. *Journal of Theoretical Politics* 6(1): 27–53.

Schatz, Florian. 2013. Fighting Corruption with Social Accountability: A Comparative Analysis of Social Accountability Mechanisms' Potential to Reduce Corruption in Public Administration. *Public Administration and Development* 33: 161–174.

Schmidt, Vivien A. 2010. Taking Ideas and Discourse Seriously: Explaining Change through Discursive Institutionalism as the Fourth "New Institutionalism." *European Political Science Review* 2(1): 1–25.

Schumpeter, Joseph A. 1934. *The Theory of Economic Development.* Cambridge, MA: Harvard University Press.

Schumpeter, Joseph A. 1947. The Study of Entrepreneurship. In *Joseph A. The Economics and Sociology of Capitalism*, ed., Richard Swedberg, 406–428. Princeton, NJ: Princeton University Press.

Selznick, Philip. 1949. *TVA and the Grass Roots: A Study in Sociology of Formal Organizations.* Berkeley, CA: University of California Press.

Simon, Herbert A. 1947. *Administrative Behavior: A Study of Decision-Making Processes in Administrative Organization.* New York: Macmillan.

Skelcher, Chris. 2012. What Do We Mean When We Talk about "Hybrids" and "Hybridity" in Public Management and Governance? Working Paper, Institute of Local Government Studies, University of Birmingham.

Sørensen, Eva. 2006. Metagovernance: The Changing Role of Politicians in Processes of Democratic Governance. *The American Review of Public Administration* 36(1): 98–114.

Sørensen, Eva, and Jacob Torfing. 2009. Making Governance Networks Effective and Democratic through Metagovernance. *Public Administration* 87: 234–258. https://doi.org/10.1111/j.1467-9299.2009.01753.x.

Sørensen, Eva, and Jacob Torfing. 2015. Enhancing Public Innovation through Collaboration, Leadership and New Public Governance. In *New Frontiers in Social Innovation Research*, eds., Alex Nicholls, Julie Simon, Madeleine Gabriel, 145–169. London: Palgrave Macmillan.

Sørensen, Eva, and Jacob Torfing. 2018. Governance on a Bumpy Road from Enfant Terrible to Mature Paradigm. *Critical Policy Studies* 12(3): 350–359.

Sørensen, Eva, and Jacob Torfing. 2021a. Accountable Government through Collaborative Governance? *Administrative Sciences* 11(4): 127.

Sørensen, Eva, and Jacob Torfing. 2021b. Radical and Disruptive Answers to Downstream Problems in Collaborative Governance? *Public Management Review* 23(11): 1590–1611.

Sorrentino Maddalena, Mariafrancesca Sicilia, and Michael Howlett. 2018. Understanding Co-production as a New Public Governance Tool. *Policy and Society* 37(3): 277–293.

Stoker, Gerry. 2006. Public Value Management: A New Narrative for Networked Governance? *The American Review of Public Administration* 36(41): 41–57.

Streeck, Wolfagang, and Katheleen Thelen. 2005. *Beyond Continuity: Institutional Change in Advanced Political Economies*. Oxford: Oxford University Press.

Svara, James H. 1994. *Facilitative Leadership in Local Government: Lessons from Successful Mayors and Chairpersons*. San Francisco, CA: Jossey-Bass.

Thomson, Ann Marie, and James L. Perry. 2006. Collaboration Processes: Inside the Black Box. *Public Administration Review* 66(s1): 20–32.

Torfing, Jacob, B. Guy Peters, Jon Pierre, and Eva Sørensen. 2012. *Interactive Governance: Advancing the Paradigm*. Oxford: Oxford Academic.

Torfing, Jacob, and Christopher Ansell. 2017. Strengthening Political Leadership and Policy Innovation through the Expansion of Collaborative Forms of Governance. *Public Management Review* 19: 37–54.

Torfing, Jacob, and Peter Triantafillou. 2013. What's in a Name? Grasping New Public Governance as a Political-Administrative System. *International Review of Public Administration* 18(2): 9–25.

Torfing, Jacob, Lotte Bøgh Andersen, Carsten Greve, and Kurt Kaudi Klausen. 2020. *Public Governance Paradigms: Competing and Co-existing*. Cheltenham: Edward Elgar.

Tsui, Ming-Sum, and Fernando C. H. Cheung. 2004. Gone with the Wind: The Impacts of Managerialism on Human Services. *British Journal of Social Work* 34: 437–442.

Van de Walle, Steven, and Gerhard Hammerschmid. 2011. The Impact of the New Public Management: Challenges for Coordination and Cohesion in European Public Sectors. *Halduskultuur–Administrative Culture* 12(2): 190–209.

van Gestel, Nicolette, Jean-Louis Denis, Ewan Ferlie, and Aoife M. McDermott. 2018. Explaining the Policy Process Underpinning Public Sector Reform: The Role of Ideas, Institutions, and Timing. *Perspectives on Public Management and Governance* 1(2): 87–101.

Van Wart, Montgomery. 2003. Public-Sector Leadership Theory: An Assessment. *Public Administration Review* 63(2): 214–228.

Van Wart, Montgomery. 2013. Administrative Leadership Theory: A Reassessment after 10 Years. *Public Administration* 91(3): 521–543.

Wagenaar, Hendrik. 2011. *Meaning in Action: Interpretation and Dialogue in Policy Analysis*. Armonk, NY: M. E. Sharpe.

Weick, Karl E., Kathleen M. Sutcliffe, and David Obstfeld. 2005. Organizing and the Process of Sensemaking. *Organization Science* 16(4): 409–421.

Weiss, Jens. 2020. The Evolution of Reform Narratives: A Narrative Policy Framework Analysis of German NPM Reforms. *Critical Policy Studies* 14(1): 106–123.

Whitehead, Mark. 2003. In the Shadow of Hierarchy: Meta-Governance, Policy, Reform and Urban Regeneration in the West Midlands. *Area* 35(1): 6–14.

Wiesel, Fredrika, and Sven Modell. 2014. From New Public Management to New Public Governance? Hybridization and Implications for Public Sector Consumerism. *Financial Accountability & Management* 30(2): 175–205.

Wise, Charles R. 2010. Organizations of the Future: Greater Hybridization Coming. *Public Administration Review* 70-supplement: 164–166.

Young, Sarah L., Kimberly K. Wiley, and Elizabeth A. M. Searing. 2020. "Squandered in Real Time": How Public Management Theory Underestimated the Public Administration–Politics Dichotomy. *The American Review of Public Administration* 50(6–7): 480–488.

Zouridis, Stavros, and Vera Leijtens. 2021. Bringing the Law Back in: The Law-Government Nexus in an Era of Network Governance. *Perspectives on Public Management and Governance* 4(2): 118–129.

Cambridge Elements ≡

Public and Nonprofit Administration

Andrew Whitford
University of Georgia

Andrew Whitford is Alexander M. Crenshaw Professor of Public Policy in the School of Public and International Affairs at the University of Georgia. His research centers on strategy and innovation in public policy and organization studies.

Robert Christensen
Brigham Young University

Robert Christensen is professor and George Romney Research Fellow in the Marriott School at Brigham Young University. His research focuses on prosocial and antisocial behaviors and attitudes in public and nonprofit organizations.

About the Series

The foundation of this series are cutting-edge contributions on emerging topics and definitive reviews of keystone topics in public and nonprofit administration, especially those that lack longer treatment in textbook or other formats. Among keystone topics of interest for scholars and practitioners of public and nonprofit administration, it covers public management, public budgeting and finance, nonprofit studies, and the interstitial space between the public and nonprofit sectors, along with theoretical and methodological contributions, including quantitative, qualitative and mixed-methods pieces.

The Public Management Research Association

The Public Management Research Association improves public governance by advancing research on public organizations, strengthening links among interdisciplinary scholars, and furthering professional and academic opportunities in public management.

Cambridge Elements ⁼

Public and Nonprofit Administration

Elements in the Series

Printed in the United States
by Baker & Taylor Publisher Services